TOO MANY CHILES!

By Dave DeWitt,
Nancy Gerlach, and Jeff Gerlach

D1316644

GOLDEN WEST COOKBOOKS

Front cover photo and assorted chiles photo on back cover by Dave DeWitt
Back cover photo of preserved chiles by Steve Tesky
Selected illustrations throughout by Lois Lyles

Dedication
To Chip Hearn,
who wanted this book.
Now the ball is in your court!

Library of Congress Cataloging-in-Publication Data
Dave DeWitt,
Too Many Chiles! : growing, using and preserving peppers/by Dave DeWitt, Nancy Gerlach, and Jeff Gerlach
p.cm.
Includes index.
ISBN 1-885590-88-1
1. Cookery (Hot peppers) 2. Hot peppers. I. Gerlach, Nancy II
Gerlach, Jeffrey III. Title
TX803.P46 D4813 2001
641.6'384—dc21   CIP
                                  2001040924

Printed in the United States of America
2013 Printing

ISBN #978-1-885590-88-6

Golden West Cookbooks
5738 North Central Avenue
Phoenix, AZ 85012-1316
800-521-9221

For free sample recipes and complete Table of Contents for every Golden West cookbook, visit our website: www.GoldenWestCookbooks.com

TABLE OF CONTENTS

INTRODUCTION

Although "too many chiles" may sound like an impossibility to some hard-core chile lovers, we'd be willing to bet that they never had to face an overwhelming chile harvest. We still remember our first really good crop, which started with a store-bought six-pack of jalapeño starter plants. Throughout the summer we irrigated and fertilized and mulched, while a wonderfully hot Albuquerque sun turned our little starter plants into good-sized bushes. Even when the plants started flowering and forming fruit, we failed to realize what was coming.

The very first pods that we picked green were turned into a fresh salsa that we immediately devoured. The next batch of pods was larger, so we made more salsa and pickled the remainder. And still the plants produced, so we pickled more and even froze some. By this time we were about "salsa'ed out," so we started giving bags away to neighbors, friends, and co-workers.

Meanwhile, the plants continued to produce into the early fall; we were simply astounded by the number of jalapeños coming from those six plants, and it wasn't too long before we started wishing that we had thrown out half of the starter plants. That experience opened our eyes to the fact that under the right conditions, chile plants are amazingly prolific, and it taught us that when growing most of the smaller varieties such as jalapeño, serrano, piquin, japones, de arbol, cayenne, or Thai, one or two plants of each are generally more than enough for our two families.

Although we have tried to practice restraint over the years, we still manage to regularly produce more than we can use, and so we have collected a great deal of information on dealing with what has become an annual deluge of chiles. From our conversations with other chile growers from all over the country, we know that many of you are also overwhelmed by your chile crops, a fact that inspired us to compile this book. If you are one of those fortunate gardeners who winds up with bushels and bushels of extra chiles, we hope that somewhere in these pages you will find a way to use those extra chiles so they won't be wasted.

For continuing coverage of gardening, harvesting, and chile recipes, be sure to check out www.fiery-foods.com on the web.

1 GROWING & HARVESTING

Hundreds of articles and at least one book—*The Pepper Garden*— have been written on the home and commercial cultivation of the Capsicums, so there's far too much information to go into great detail in this section. This chapter is designed as a basic gardening guide for beginners using organic techniques.

THE STRATEGY

The combination of long growing times of the increasingly popular exotic chile varieties and the medium to short growing seasons in many parts of North America forces many gardeners to examine their strategy. In order to get the maximum number of peppers from these potentially prolific varieties, the plants need enough time to produce and ripen up the pods. That often means extending the natural growing season at the front end, the back end, or both.

STARTING SEEDS

To stretch the beginning of the pepper growing season, start the plants indoors around January or February. Sow the pepper seeds in "recycled" plastic six-packs (from plants bought at nurseries) filled with a loose seed-starting mix. Plant far more seeds than the actual number of plants needed for the garden, thinning out the weakest plants later, and perhaps even planting a few of the extra seedlings in pots that can be moved back indoors come fall.

After sowing the seeds in the pre-moistened seed-starting mix, set the six-packs (or seed-starting flat or pots or whatever) on a source of bottom heat (such as a heating cable, a seed-starting mat, or the top of the refrigerator) to boost germination. Cover the setup loosely with plastic to retain moisture, spritz the surface lightly with tepid water every day if it seems dry, and then, after the seeds have sprouted, remove the plastic and move the containers someplace where the

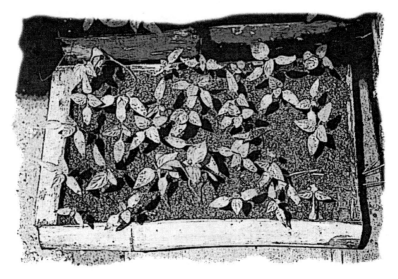

seedlings will receive plenty of bright light—either the sill of a super-bright, clean window; very close to a four tube fluorescent fixture; or under some high-intensity grow lights.

The pepper plants will grow more foliage and flowers (and therefore more fruit) if the seedlings are prevented from becoming rootbound. So transplant them into increasingly larger pots, starting when the seedlings hit the four-leaf stage. Then, when the seedlings are finally transplanted outside, their roots will be vigorous and spread out—not cramped—and the plants will get off to a running start.

Pests

A couple of pests do go after pepper seedlings—aphids especially like to attack young plants indoors. Fight these little pests by knocking the aphids off the seedlings with a spray mixture of soapy water and chile powder. To make it, add about one-half to one teaspoon of the hottest, most finely ground chile powder to a quart of ready-made insecticidal soap solution (mixed according to the label) or to a quart of water containing 2 drops of dishwashing soap, well mixed.

The other "pest" most known for its tendency to damage pepper seedlings (and thus reducing potential yields) is a cat, who will graze on your pepper seedlings if he/she has the chance, so keep the six-packs and seedling tray out of reach.

TRANSPLANTING

Soon the pampered peppers will be moved from the protected sanctuary of the home or greenhouse into the brutal spring environment of high winds, low temperatures, and bright light. To strengthen the seedlings' stems so that they can withstand those outdoor winds, place them in front of a fan for 3 to 7 days before they are scheduled to go outside. Keep the fan on day and night at a setting that's just high enough to create a moderate breeze. Don't blow the seedlings over—just create some good air circulation.

Then sometimes around the last frost date, begin to further prepare the seedlings for their move outdoors by "hardening them off." Place the seedlings outside in semi-shade for increasing periods of time each day—even overnight if a nice warm spell hits—over a 1 to 2 week period.

PREPARING THE PLOT

While hardening off those seedlings, prepare their future garden site. They'll grow best in raised beds in most regions and in sunken beds in dry climates. The pepper garden should ideally be located somewhere that peppers haven't grown for several years to help prevent disease problems. Admittedly, a strict crop rotation is hard to do in a small garden, but a pepper planting can at least follow a spring crop of peas. Try not to grow peppers in the same spot two years in a row.

Dig some compost or aged manure into the pepper bed before planting. Use aged (not fresh) manure to ensure against nitrogen overdose, which can cause low pod yields. There have been cases of six foot tall jalapeño plants with plenty of foliage but no pods on them because the grower fed them too much nitrogen.

If growing peppers in the North (or any place where the ground is chilly), warm up the soil by covering it with black plastic for a few days before the planting. Don't pull up this "mulch" later on—leave it right where it is and plant the peppers into holes cut into the plastic—this will keep the soil warm, decrease the water needs, and prevent weeds.

When planting, use only the healthiest and most vigorous seedlings. Leggy, stunted or aphid-damaged plants will not recover

sufficiently to fulfill their yield potential. Space the seedlings about 6 to 12 inches apart. Many garden guidelines suggest a 12-inch spacing between pepper plants, but smaller-podded varieties can easily be squeezed into a 6-inch space.

But don't plant all of the seedlings in the ground. Save some of the plants for growing in containers outside, so the pots can be moved indoors to a brightly lit area when the weather turns cool in the fall.

The newly transplanted peppers will need as much warmth as they can get. Protect the peppers from low temperatures by covering the plants with a floating row cover, such as Reemay. Some gardeners surround their seedlings with water-filled inner tubes or Wallo'Waters (flexible plastic tubes arranged in a circle that are filled with water, sold at garden centers, nurseries and by mail-order). The water absorbs heat from the sun during the day, and then holds onto that heat after temperatures start to cool. Overnight, the water releases that heat, keeping the soil and air around the seedlings nice and warm. Another warm-water technique is to fill several gallon-sized plastic milk jugs with water and bury them halfway in the ground next to each seedling (be careful not to disturb the plant's roots when digging).

HABANERO

THE GROWING SEASON

When summer arrives, weeds may try to seize control of the pepper patch. Prevent them at all costs. Weeds not only look ugly, they can harbor pests like leafhoppers, which spread curly top virus to pepper plants (which happened with devastating effect throughout New Mexico in 1995). So keep those hoppers homeless by keeping the garden weed-free.

For gardeners who live in warm zones, the summer sun can be more of a hindrance than a help to getting high yields. Intense sunlight can actually cook peppers (a problem called sunscald) and decrease the yield of usable fruits. If gardening in a high-altitude region with intense sunlight, shade the peppers by covering the plants with shade netting (available at garden centers or by mail order). Rig up a makeshift frame over the peppers and drape the shade cloth over this frame so it remains easy to tend the peppers under their "tent." Varieties such as habaneros and rocotos are especially prone to sunscald, and both yield better under the netting than they do in open, unshaded plots.

During the hottest days of July and August, pepper plants can lose a lot of water through their leaves (transpiration). When this occurs, the leaves wilt and the flowers (and sometimes fruit) drop right off the plants. Reduce this water loss by boosting the humidity around the plants with a thick layer of mulch, if using it). If using organic techniques, fertilize the plants with fish emulsion. Otherwise, use a mild, diluted solution of water soluble fertilizer, taking care not to over-fertilize.

Once the plants start producing their peppers, there's another little trick to use to maximize the yields—at least with the pepper varieties that are eaten green, such as jalapeños, serranos, and the New Mexican varieties. Increase the total yield of these varieties by continually picking the peppers when they reach their largest "mature green" size, and not waiting for them to fully ripen on the plant. When a pepper plant reaches its "fruit load" (the maximum weight of peppers the plant can support), it will stop flowering and fruiting even though there may be a month or more left in the growing season. Removing the mature green fruits signal the plant to continue flowering and setting fruit throughout the remainder of the season—and the result is more pods per plant.

HARVEST TIME

Often, the first frost of the year does not signal the end of the growing season. The early frost is followed by an "Indian Summer" that brings enough warm weather to keep peppers growing for another 3 or 4 weeks. But to make use of this extended season, it is necessary to cover the plants. There are many good crop protectors—cotton bed sheets, clear or black plastic, nylon netting, plastic row covers, even large cardboard boxes placed over individual plants. The material should be thick and dense enough to retain ground heat, but not so thick that it will break off branches if it gets weighted down by rain or snow.

Place the covers in position as early in the day as possible—say between 4 and 6 p.m. on the evening of the frost—so that there's still some heat to retain (it gets cool fast at night in the fall). And be sure to remove such covers as soon as it's warm enough the following day.

If the temperature is going to drop below 28 degrees F though, the covering efforts will probably not be enough to protect the plants from the cold. But there are other plants, those peppers that have been growing in pots. Move them indoors before the first frost, and the plants will overwinter nicely. If there are not any peppers in pots, dig up a few of the healthiest favorites in the garden (don't dig up a struggler hoping it'll recover inside—it won't), pot them in a soil that drains well and move them inside. These plants may drop most of their leaves over the winter, but most will survive and come back strong—especially if they are pruned in the spring, cutting off any branches that look dead and brown, rather than green. The plants will sprout new growth vigorously after such a pruning, even if you cut them back severely.

Gardeners can even make this indoor overwintering and spring pruning a perennial event because peppers are perennials when grown in frost-free conditions. Wintered-over pepper plants need regular watering, but unless you are actively growing them by providing artificial light, there is no need to fertilize them until they resume growing in the spring.

CAYENNE

HARVESTING & PROCESSING

As mentioned previously, pepper gardening experts recommend the technique of staggered harvesting, which means that the chiles in the garden can be used all season long. Usually the first chiles available are those which are small and used green in fresh salsas—the serranos, jalapeños, and the young green pods of other varieties such as the habanero.

Some chiles, especially the New Mexican varieties, can be eaten or processed as soon as they are about four inches long, or they can be allowed to turn red before picking and drying. However, there are a few varieties that are generally used only in their dried state, such as cayenne and pasilla chiles.

It is important to continue harvesting the ripe pods as they mature. The best time to pick chiles for drying is when they first start to turn red. This timing will stimulate the plant into further production, and the harvested chiles can be strung to dry and will turn bright red.

Haphazard harvesting can result in waste, so careful plucking is essential to ensure the maximum yield of the chile pepper patch. Choose pods which have smooth, shiny skins and are firm to the touch. A good rule to follow is that if the pod comes off the stem

easily, the chile is ready. If you have to tug on the pod, it is too early to pick it. The small chiles do not have to be peeled or processed in any way before being used. They can be picked, washed, and used in any recipe.

Drying is the oldest and most common way to preserve chile pods and works well for most chiles—except the very meaty ones such as jalapeños, which are smoke-dried and called chipotle. For hundreds of years, New Mexicans have been stringing chiles onto ristras (strings) and hanging them in the sun to dry. See Chapter 5 for details on drying.

FOR CHILE HANDLING TIPS, REFER TO CAUTIONARY NOTES ON PAGE 20

EXCESS CHILES

If, after using the techniques in this book, you still have more pods than you can use, here are a few suggestions. Despite the fact that many of our friends and neighbors also grow chiles, we have found that most people grow only one or two of their favorite varieties, and therefore are quite happy to accept bags of new or different chiles. In addition, we realize that the majority of people out there do not garden, and if we can make contact with them, they will generally be thrilled to take any excess. Organizations that provide food for the homeless generally are happy to accept donations of homegrown produce, although they obviously have limits on the number of hot chiles that they can use or accept.

Over the years, we have found a number of trading partners who know that we always grow chiles, and as a result, plant few, if any chiles of their own. Instead, they rely on us to provide them with chiles, while we in turn rely on them to supply fruits or vegetables that we are unwilling or unable to grow. This works especially well for any plant or variety that tends to overproduce, such as full-sized fruit trees. We are always happy to trade our extra chiles, for say fresh pears or peaches, neither of which we grow.

In addition, it is also possible to sell your surplus. These days, nearly every town has a grower's market of some kind. Here in Albuquerque, we have several neighborhood markets in the city which are open on weekends. For a minimal fee, growers are allowed to set up a table and sell their crops. So, if you have extra chiles and a half day or so to "man" your table, you can generally sell all your homegrown produce.

Our primary concern at these markets is to find a home for our excess, not to get rich. We usually keep our prices low enough to guarantee that we walk away empty-handed, and find that most buyers are excited and enthusiastic about finding really fresh produce at good prices. We also find that these markets are a good place to trade, and often wind up with a load of traded goods, but little or no money. Any money that we do earn goes towards buying either more seeds or other gardening products.

2 FRESH FROM THE GARDEN

Most of us love chiles in whatever form we can get them, but there is something special about fresh chiles. There is a taste and a texture that cannot be duplicated by canned, dried, or frozen chiles, and they also add such bright colors to summertime meals. So naturally, the first way to handle a mega-harvest, is to consume as many of the fresh chiles as possible.

There are many ways to use fresh chiles straight from the garden. Obviously, they can just be eaten, although many of the smaller, hotter varieties are simply too hot to be eaten straight. We love to slice up a batch of hot chiles and use them fresh on sandwiches as well as on hot dogs and burgers. They can also be used in salads of all kinds.

As you can see from the following recipes, there are many other ways to use fresh chiles that require little or no cooking, as well as being fast and easy to prepare. We also include a number of recipes for cooked sauces and salsas, as well as cooked dishes that use fresh chiles.

ROASTING AND PEELING CHILES

Certain large fresh chiles, such as New Mexico green chiles and poblano chiles, have a tough outer skin that must be removed before using. The only practical way to remove the skin is to apply heat to the chile so that the skin blisters and pulls away from the meat of the chile. It then becomes easy to peel off the skin. There are several different methods of blistering chiles, and all of them work well. The decision on how to blister depends on what kind of equipment is available, as well as the number of chiles to be blistered.

The first step is to choose your heat source. Oven broilers work well, but seem to require sitting on the floor for extended periods of time if you're working with any quantity of chile. We recommend that you get the chile right up under the flame or you'll be there for a day or two trying to roast even 10 pounds. Stove top burners (both

gas and electric) also do a good job if covered with some heavy wire mesh. We recommend using a stove top grill which is made especially for this purpose. The drawback here is the small number of chiles that can be blistered at one time. We use this heat source frequently when we have just a few chiles to roast.

Outdoor grills are one of the best ways to roast chiles. It is easy to regulate the heat, and a large number of chiles can be blistered at the same time. We like to make an event out of our chile roasting; we fire up the charcoal or gas grill, chill down a six-pack, turn on some music, and spend an afternoon roasting our winter supply. Chile roasters, which are usually not available outside of New Mexico or the Southwest, are the fastest and easiest of all. These machines feature a squirrel-type cage for the chiles along with one or more burners hooked into a tank of propane. Larger models are motor driven. If using a roaster, we recommend that the chiles be blistered slowly which will allow the chile's natural sugar to caramelize, and improve the chile's taste.

Once you've decided on your heat source, it's time to start the heat and prepare the chiles. If they need it, wash off the chiles and let them dry. This will prevent any dust or dirt from getting on the edible part of the chile when they are peeled. Cut a small slit in the side of each chile before placing it on the fire. If you forget this step, the chiles will remind you by exploding with a loud pop, shooting their seeds (some of which can be very hot!) five or six feet in every direction. Not every chile will do this, but it is a good idea to keep a knife handy and simply stab every chile as you throw it on the fire.

As you roast the chiles, keep flipping them over to make sure that they are not burning. You will actually be able to see the skin blistering—even blackening somewhat—and pulling away from the meat of the chile. Whether or not you see that occur, it is important to brown virtually the entire chile in order to easily remove the skin. Don't be timid—the chiles can take a lot of heat before burning. On the other hand, we are merely blistering the chiles, not incinerating them.

After the chiles are well-blistered, place them in a large bowl and cover with a damp towel. This will "steam" the chiles a bit, and will make peeling them infinitely easier. Or, you can place the hot roasted chiles in a heavy plastic bag which will ensure easy peeling. Allow the

chiles to cool off under the towel or in the bag (30 to 90 minutes) and peeling will be a breeze. You can also avoid scorching your fingers because blistered chiles right off the grill are hot little critters! For crisper chiles, plunge them into ice water after roasting. This will stop any further cooking of the roasted pods.

After the chiles have cooled down, it's time for the final step. If you've done a good job of roasting your chiles, peeling them is fast and easy. Simply start at either end, and pull off the skin. We generally pull from the tip back towards the stem, but it depends on the roasting job. Occasionally, you will run into problems with the deep indentations; it is hard to blister those "valleys" without burning the surrounding areas. In these cases, you simply have to go in with a knife and scrape off any remaining skin.

Because the hotter varieties of green chile are thinner fleshed than the mild ones, it is difficult to peel them and come up with an intact pod. They tend to tear and split apart during the peeling process. If you are going to chop the chile before using, it really doesn't matter if the pods split. If you want chiles to stuff, however, this can be a disaster. To produce intact, roasted and peeled green chile pods, simply start with mild chile pods, which have much thicker flesh.

At this point, most people like to cut off the stem and remove the seeds. The easiest method is to simply cut off the very top of the chile

along with the stem, and then scrape the seeds out of the open end. Removing the seeds will cause a slight loss of pungency because they are attached to the placental tissue. If you really want to reduce the firepower, you can also remove the veins (the placental tissue) that run the length of the chile and serve to attach the seeds to the pod. You've now completed the whole process and have a chile that is ready to eat, cook or freeze.

FResH ReD CHiLe

Most chile lovers are familiar with New Mexico green chiles, which are the large (5" to 10"), fleshy, mild chiles that are also called Anaheim chiles. (Anaheim is actually a variety of New Mexico chiles, as are Sandia, Big Jim, etc.) These same green chiles are the immature stage of the New Mexico red chiles, which are used to make chile ristras, and when dried, are ground into red chile powder. There is a stage between fresh green and dried red that is known as fresh red, and many people swear that this is the most delicious stage. It has a fresh taste like fresh green, but also includes the rich flavor of dried red pods. For those who have never tried it, it is a deliciously new chile flavor sensation.

Green chile, like many other chiles, undergoes a substantial chemical transformation as it turns red and matures, as the sugars and vitamin A increase. As soon as the pods turn red, they start to dry out. Fresh red is the stage where the pods have just turned red, and are as fat and sassy as fresh green. In fact, fresh red is handled just like fresh green—that is, roasted and peeled. Many people use fresh red just like fresh green, for chiles rellenos, red chile stew, and chop it to eat on sandwiches, steaks, hamburgers, and eggs, just to name a few. Personally, we prefer to use fresh green for most of those foods; we use fresh red to prepare a base for some wonderfully tasty red chile sauces.

CAUTIONARY NOTES

Capsaicin, the alkaloid responsible for the heat in chiles, is a joy in food—it hurts so good! It is far less welcome in large doses on the skin, or in any amount in an eye. We urge everyone who works with or processes chile in any quantity to wear gloves while handling the chile. This is especially important when handling the hottest varieties because chile burns can be extremely painful, which we can testify to from personal experience. They are also nearly impossible to cure; about the only thing to do is to wait them out because they will eventually wear off.

If you do get burned, remember that capsaicin is oil soluble, meaning that water will have no affect on it. So if you come down with Hunan hand, which is the official name for capsaicin-burned hands, the best remedy is to coat your hands in vegetable oil, rather than soap and water. Even this will not completely eliminate the heat, but it will reduce it. (The same advice applies to flaming taste buds; rather than water, consume a dairy product such as sour cream, yogurt, or ice cream.)

In addition, be careful where you put your nose while cooking chile. It's not wise to stick your nose right over the top of the blender as you remove the lid after grinding up a batch of chiles, likewise with a covered pot of chiles that is being cooked on the stove. Whenever you're working with or cooking chiles, it's a good idea to keep your face away from any concentrated chile combinations.

SALSA FRESCA

Fresh salsas during the summer are a great way to use the earliest pods such as jalapeños and serranos. Vary the flavor of the salsa by using different chiles as they become available. Keep a supply on hand to serve with chips as a dip, as an accompaniment to grilled poultry or fish, or with burritos, fajitas, or even hamburgers. This salsa will keep for 2 days in the refrigerator.

3 **Serrano** or **Jalapeño Chiles**, stems and seeds removed, minced
2 **Yellow Wax Chiles**, stems and seeds removed, minced
2 large **Tomatoes**, finely diced
1 medium **Purple Onion**, finely diced
2 cloves **Garlic**, minced
2 tablespoons **Vegetable Oil**
2 tablespoons fresh **Lime Juice** or **Cider Vinegar**
1/4 cup chopped fresh **Cilantro** or **Parsley**
1 large **Avocado**, diced

Combine all the ingredients except the cilantro and avocado, and let the salsa sit for at least 1 hour to blend the flavors.

Mix in the cilantro and avocado before serving.

Yield: 2 cups   *Heat Scale: Medium*

CARIBBEAN SALSA

The combination of fresh fruit and chile produces a salsa that goes well with lighter fare such as grilled chicken or fish. This will keep for up to a week in the refrigerator.

- 1 cup diced fresh **Mango**
- 1 cup diced fresh **Papaya**
- 6 **Serrano Chiles**, stems removed, minced or substitute 2 habaneros
- 1/2 **Red Bell Pepper**, stem and seeds removed, minced
- 3 **Green Onions**, sliced, including some of the green
- 1/4 cup fresh **Lime Juice**
- 2 tablespoons **Vegetable Oil**
- Chopped fresh **Cilantro**

Combine all the ingredients and allow to sit for 1 hour to blend the flavors.

Yield: 2 cups   *Heat Scale: Hot*

LOUISIANA-STYLE HOT SAUCE

This very easy to prepare sauce only gets better as it ages. Allow it to sit for at least a week before using, if possible. For a green version of this sauce, use serrano, jalapeño, or Thai chiles in their green stage, instead of the red varieties called for below.

Note: This recipe requires advance preparation.

- 1/2 cup fresh **Tabasco Chiles**, stems removed, or substitute cayenne, piquín, or japones chiles
- 2/3 cup **White Vinegar**
- 1 3/4 teaspoons **Salt**

Place all the ingredients in a blender or food processor and purée until smooth.

Pour into a clean, sterilized bottle and let steep in the refrigerator for a few weeks before using.

Yield: 3/4 to 1 cup   *Heat Scale: Hot*

New Mexican Green Chile Sauce

This versatile sauce is basic to New Mexican cuisine. It is best with freshly roasted and peeled chile but can be made with canned, frozen or even dried green chile. Finely diced pork can be added, but cook the sauce for an additional half hour. Use this sauce over enchiladas, burritos, or tacos. It will keep for about 5 days in the refrigerator and freezes well.

- 1 small **Onion**, finely chopped
- 1 clove **Garlic**, minced
- 2 tablespoons **Vegetable Oil**
- 1 tablespoon **All-Purpose Flour**
- 2 to 3 cups **Chicken Broth**
- 1 cup chopped **New Mexico Green Chile**, roasted, peeled, stems removed
- 1 small **Tomato**, peeled and chopped

Sauté the onion and garlic in the oil until soft. Stir in the flour and blend well. Simmer the mixture for a couple of minutes to "cook" the flour. Slowly add the broth and stir the sauce until smooth.

Add the remaining ingredients, bring to a boil, reduce the heat, and simmer until the sauce has thickened, about 15 minutes.

Yield: 2 to 3 cups   *Heat Scale: Medium*

**NEW
MEXICO
GREEN**

FRESH RED CHILE SAUCE

This method of making chile sauce differs from others using fresh New Mexico chiles because these chiles aren't roasted and peeled first. Because of the high sugar content of fresh red chiles, this sauce is sweeter than most. We harvested some chiles from the garden one late summer day, made a batch of this sauce, and ate every drop as a soup! It makes a tasty enchilada sauce, too. It will keep for about a week in the refrigerator.

1/4 cup **Vegetable Oil**
8 fresh **New Mexico Red Chiles** (or more to taste), seeds and stems removed, chopped
1 large **Onion**, chopped
3 cloves **Garlic**, chopped
4 cups **Water**
1/4 teaspoon **Ground Cumin**
1 tablespoon minced fresh **Cilantro**
1/2 teaspoon dried **Oregano**, Mexican preferred
Salt to taste

Heat the oil in a large saucepan and sauté the chiles, onion, and garlic until the onion is soft, about 7 minutes.

Add the remaining ingredients, bring to a boil, then reduce the heat and simmer for 1 hour, uncovered.

In a blender, purée the sauce in batches and return it to the saucepan. Cook until the sauce thickens to the desired consistency. Add salt to taste.

Yield: About 3 cups   *Heat Scale: Mild to Medium*

ASIAN CHILE PASTE

Popular throughout Southeast Asia, this garlic and chile based paste is used as a condiment that adds fire without greatly altering the taste of the dish. It is especially good in stir-frys. To use up a lot of chiles, triple the recipe. It will keep for up to 3 months in the refrigerator. It can also be frozen.

1 cup small fresh **Red Chiles**, stems removed, such as Thai, Serrano, piquín, or japones
1/3 cup **White Vinegar**
8 cloves **Garlic**, chopped
3 tablespoons **Vegetable Oil**
1 teaspoon **Salt**

Combine all the ingredients in a blender or food processor and purée, adding water a little bit at a time, to form a thick paste.

Yield: 1 cup   *Heat Scale: Hot*

TROPICAL SHERRY SAUCE

This recipe is similar to a very popular Jamaican product that uses alcohol as a base. The longer the sauce steeps, the hotter it will become, so remove the chiles when the sauce has reached the desired heat level. Use the sauce over fried chicken or seafood. The tamarind sauce is available in Asian and Latin markets. This sauce will keep for several weeks in the refrigerator.

Note: This recipe requires advance preparation

2 **Habanero Chiles**, stems and seeds removed, coarsely chopped
1/2 cup dry **Sherry**
1/4 cup **Catsup**
3 tablespoons **Soy Sauce**

2 tablespoons **Lime Juice**
1 tablespoon **Tamarind Sauce**
1 tablespoon **Brown Sugar**
1 1/2 teaspoons **Dry Hot Mustard Powder**

Combine all the ingredients in a bowl, cover, and allow to steep in the refrigerator for a week to 10 days to blend the flavors.

Yield: 1 1/2 cups   *Heat Scale: Hot*

Belizean-Style Habanero Hot Sauce

In order to preserve the distinctive flavor of the habanero chiles, we add them after cooking the other ingredients of this delicious, but fiery hot sauce. To cut the heat, add more carrots or decrease the number of chiles. To use up a lot of habaneros, triple the recipe as this sauce will keep for months in the refrigerator.

1 small **Onion**, chopped
1 tablespoon **Vegetable Oil**
1 cup chopped **Carrots**
4 **Habanero Chiles**, stems and seeds removed, minced
3 tablespoons **Lime Juice**, fresh preferred
3 tablespoons **White Vinegar**
1 teaspoon **Salt**

Sauté the onion in the oil in a saucepan until soft. Add the carrots and 2 cups of water. Bring to a boil, reduce the heat and simmer until the carrots are soft. Remove from the heat.

Add the chiles, lime juice, vinegar, and salt to the carrot mixture. Place in a blender or food processor and purée until smooth. Pour into sterilized bottles and close with lids.

Yield: 2 cups   *Heat Scale: Hot*

Santaka

Mexi-Bell

Rocoto

Cayenne

FRESH RED CHILE PASTE

This easy to prepare, tasty paste provides a fresh flavor to any dish you make. You can also cook this up in large batches and freeze it for use all year long. The paste is very versatile and can be used as a base for enchilada sauces or chili con carne, or as an ingredient in marinades or pasta sauces. It will keep for a week in the refrigerator, or you can freeze it in small batches.

12 fresh **New Mexico Red Chiles**, roasted, peeled, stems and seeds removed
2 cloves **Garlic**
1/2 teaspoon **Salt**

Place all the ingredients in a blender or food processor with just enough water to blend. Purée until smooth, adding water if necessary; the paste should be thick.

Strain to remove any fibers from the paste.

Variation: Add more liquid and make a sauce.

Yield: 3/4 to 1 cup   *Heat Scale: Medium*

SEAFOOD STUFFED JALAPEÑOS

Serve these chilled as an appetizer or even as a luncheon entrée on blistering hot summer days. The jalapeños can also be roasted and peeled before using in this recipe.

1 4.5-ounce can **Crab Meat**
1 4.5-ounce can **Salad Shrimp**, chopped
1/3 cup grated **Monterey Jack Cheese**
Mayonnaise
8 to 10 fresh **Jalapeño**s, stems and seeds removed, split in half lengthwise

Combine the crab, shrimp, and cheese. Add enough mayonnaise so the stuffing holds together and mix well. Fill the jalapeño halves with a mound of the mixture.

Serve immediately or chill well before serving.

Yield: 16 to 20 stuffed jalapeño halves   *Heat Scale: Hot*

SPICY PEPPER PASTA SALAD

This salad is excellent as a lunch entrée or as an accompaniment to a larger meal. The feta cheese, yogurt, and dried oregano give it a Mediterranean flavor.

3 tablespoons **Red Wine Vinegar**
3 tablespoons **Olive Oil**
2 tablespoons **Plain Yogurt**
1 clove **Garlic**, minced
4 **Yellow Wax Chiles**, stems and seeds removed, chopped
4 cups cooked **Rotini Spiral Pasta**
12 cherry **Tomatoes**, cut in half
1/2 cup sliced **Cucumber**
1/3 cup chopped **Purple Onion**
1/4 cup sliced **Black Olives**
1/2 cup **Feta Cheese**, crumbled
1 tablespoon dried **Oregano**

To make the dressing, combine the vinegar, oil, yogurt, and garlic in bowl and mix well.

Toss the dressing with the remaining ingredients in another bowl and refrigerate until thoroughly chilled. Lightly toss again before serving.

Yield: 4 to 6 servings   *Heat Scale: Mild*

ANCHO

A mature, dried poblano, it is dark reddish-brown and wrinkled. This chile has a mild, almost fruity flavor and is the best-known and most widely-used dried chile in the United States.

CHILES RELLENOS

All fresh New Mexico green chiles are great for stuffing, but we prefer Big Jims because they are so large. Fresh poblano chiles (a Mexican favorite) and even large jalapeños can also be used. Top the rellenos with either a red or green chile sauce before serving.

6 **New Mexico Green Chiles**, roasted and peeled, stems left on
Cheddar or **Monterey Jack Cheese**, cut in sticks
All-Purpose Flour for dredging
3 **Eggs**, separated
1 tablespoon **Water**
3 tablespoons **Flour**
1/4 teaspoon **Salt**
Vegetable Oil for frying

Make a slit in the side of each chile and stuff them with the cheese. Dredge the chiles in the flour and set aside.

In a bowl, whip the egg whites until they form stiff peaks. In another bowl, beat the yolks with the water, flour, and salt until thick and creamy. Fold the yolks into the whites to make the batter.

Pour the oil into a frying pan to a depth of an inch and a half and heat to 375 degrees F. Dip the chiles into the batter and fry, turning once, until a golden brown.

Yield: 3 servings   *Heat Scale: Medium*

POBLANO

One of the most popular stuffing chiles, the poblano is large, dark green, and triangular-shaped. The thickness of its skin makes it particularly easy to stuff without tearing.

ENCHILADAS WITH RED CHILE PASTE

Using the chile paste as a basis for your red chile sauce gives a new taste dimension to your enchiladas.

- 1 cup **Red Chile Paste** (see recipe page 27)
- 2 cups **Water** or **Chicken Broth**
- 1/4 teaspoon **Ground Cumin**
- 1/4 cup **Vegetable Oil**
- 6 to 8 **Corn Tortillas**
- 2 cups cooked, shredded **Chicken**
- 2 cups grated **Asadero** or **Monterey Jack Cheese**
- 1 small **Onion**, chopped

Preheat the oven to 350 degrees F.

Combine the chile paste, water, and cumin in a pan. Bring to a boil, reduce the heat and simmer until the sauce has thickened.

Heat the oil in a skillet. When the oil is hot, quickly dip the tortillas into the oil one at a time, for a couple of seconds to soften. Remove and drain on a paper towel.

Place a couple of tablespoons of the sauce in the bottom of a casserole dish or baking pan. Dip a tortilla in the sauce and place in the pan. Put some of the chicken, cheese, and onion in the tortilla and roll up, placing the seam on the bottom. Continue with the procedure until the pan is full.

Pour the remaining sauce over the top and bake for 15 to 20 minutes or until hot. Garnish with additional grated cheese before serving.

Yield: 3 to 4 servings   *Heat Scale: Medium*

Texas Ranchero Sauce

This "ranch-style" sauce is one of the most popular sauces in the state of Texas. It is commonly served over eggs on tortillas to make huevos rancheros. Some versions replace the bell peppers with poblanos or New Mexican green chiles. This will keep for about three days in the refrigerator, but it also freezes well.

3 fresh **Jalapeño Chiles**, seeds and stems removed, finely chopped
2 green **Bell Peppers**, seeds and stems removed, finely chopped
1 medium **Onion**, minced
2 cloves **Garlic**, minced
1/4 cup **Vegetable Oil**
4 to 6 ripe **Tomatoes**, quartered
1/2 teaspoon **Mexican Oregano**
Salt and **Pepper** to taste

In a saucepan, sauté the chiles, bell peppers, onion, and garlic until the onion is soft, about 7 minutes. In a food processor, process the tomatoes to a coarse paste. Add the tomatoes to the chile mixture, add the oregano and simmer for about 30 minutes or until the sauce is thickened to the desired consistency.

Yield: 3 to 4 cups   *Heat Scale: Medium*

CHILES RELLENOS CON RES Y PASA

(BEEF AND RAISIN-STUFFED CHILES)

This recipe was collected in Aguascalientes, which received this name because it is close to thermal springs. This stuffed chile recipe is unusual in that the chiles are not battered and fried. Thus the pure flavor of the roasted poblano chiles shines through.

1 pound **Beef Roast**
1 clove **Garlic**, chopped
1/2 teaspoon **Salt**
1/2 **Onion**, chopped
1 tablespoon **Vegetable Oil**
1 cup chopped Tomato
1 tablespoon **Vinegar**
10 **Olives**, chopped
20 **Raisins**, chopped
10 **Almonds**, peeled and chopped
6 **Poblano Chiles**, roasted, peeled, seeds removed through a slit
    below the stem, stems left on
1/2 cup **Cream**
Cilantro Leaves for garnish

Boil the meat in a large pot in water to cover with the garlic and salt. Once the meat is cooked, remove it from the pot and shred it.

Heat the oil in a skillet, and sauté the onion until soft. Add the tomato and vinegar and fry a while longer. Then add the meat and stir. Add the olives, raisins, almonds and salt to taste. Stuff the chiles with this mixture through the slit and place them in the oven on a greased cookie sheet. Bake at 350 degrees for 10 minutes. Heat the cream in a pan and drizzle the cream evenly over each chile as it is served. Garnish with the cilantro leaves.

Yield: 6 servings   *Heat Scale: Mild*

HOMEMADE TABASCO®-STYLE SAUCE

The United States has become one of the world's largest producers of hot sauces, and the flagship of the hot sauce fleet is Tabasco®, which is exported all over the world from Avery Island, Louisiana. Because the chiles in mash form are not aged in oak barrels for three years, this recipe will be only a rough approximation of the famous McIlhenny product. You will have to grow your own tabascos or substitute dried ones that have been rehydrated. Other small, hot, fresh red chiles can also be substituted for the tabascos.
Note: This recipe requires advance preparation.

1 pound fresh **Red Tabasco Chiles**, chopped	2 cups distilled **White Vinegar**
	2 teaspoons **Salt**

Combine the chiles and vinegar in a saucepan and heat. Stir in the salt and simmer for 5 minutes. Remove from the heat, let cool, and transfer to a blender. Purée until smooth. Transfer the mixture to a glass jar. Allow to steep for 2 weeks in the refrigerator. Strain the sauce, and adjust the consistency by adding more vinegar if necessary.

Yield: 2 cups   *Heat Scale: Hot*

MANGO FANDANGO SALSA

From chef and cookbook author Jay Solomon comes a fruity, tropical twist on traditional salsa. "The sweet, luscious flavor of mango is wonderfully juxtaposed with the searing bite of the Scotch bonnet," he told us.

1 ripe **Mango**, peeled, pitted, and diced
1/4 cup minced **Red Onion**
1 **Scotch Bonnet Chile**, seeds and stem removed, minced
2 tablespoons **Lime Juice**
1 tablespoon minced fresh **Cilantro**
1/4 ground **Cumin**
1/4 teaspoon **White Pepper**
1/4 teaspoon **Salt**

Combine all of the ingredients in a bowl and mix thoroughly. Refrigerate for 1 hour. Serve with grilled fish, chicken, or lamb.

Yield: 2 cups   *Heat Scale: Hot*

Keeping "Pace®" with Picante Sauces

Although most commercial salsas and picante sauces are made from similar ingredients, their flavors differ because of the spices, cooking techniques, and proportion of ingredients used in each recipe. Perhaps this home-cooked version outdoes the original of the best-selling American salsa—you tell me. It is important to use only Mexican oregano, as Mediterranean oregano will make this taste like a pasta sauce.

6 to 8 ripe **Red Tomatoes** (about 4 pounds), peeled, seeded, and chopped fine

2 **Onions**, peeled and chopped

3 cloves **Garlic**, peeled and minced

1 cup **Apple Cider Vinegar**

2 teaspoons **Mexican Oregano**

1 tablespoon **Tomato Paste**

Salt to taste

6 **Jalapeño Chiles**, stems and seeds removed, chopped very fine

In a large saucepan or Dutch oven, combine the tomatoes, onions, garlic, vinegar, oregano, tomato paste, and salt. Bring to a boil, reduce the heat to medium, and cook for 15 to thicken the sauce.

Add the jalapeños and continue cooking for 15 more minutes. Remove from the heat, cool to room temperature, and serve with chips.

Yield: About 4 cups   *Heat Scale: Medium*

3. CANNED CAPSICUMS

Generally speaking, canning is not the best way to preserve chiles at home. But over the years, so many people have asked us how to do it that we have compiled the following information. Canned chiles, especially the New Mexican varieties, are readily available in supermarkets.

PRESSURE CANNING

Because they are a low-acid fruit, chiles canned at home must be pressure canned to be safe. If improperly done, botulism can develop. Therefore, home canning of chiles is not to be considered unless one has a pressure canner. If you have the proper equipment, follow the manufacturer's instructions to the letter to ensure safe results. The following description will take you through the basic steps, but again, it is imperative that the instructions for each particular canner be followed.

To begin, blister and peel large chiles, and if desired, remove stems and seeds from all chiles used. (See Chapter 2 for roasting and peeling instructions.) Pack the prepared chile loosely into hot, clean jars, leaving an inch of head room. Add salt (1/4 teaspoon/half pint, 1/2 teaspoon/pint) and add boiling water up to the one inch head room level. Put on lids, tighten well, and place in the canner according to manufacturer's directions.

After letting steam escape from the canner for 10 minutes, close the petcock and process 1/2 pints for 30 minutes, pints for 35 minutes. When finished, remove the canner from the heat and let the pressure fall to zero, which will take up to half an hour. When the pressure reaches zero, open the petcock, wait 5 minutes, then open the canner and remove the jars to a draft-free location to cool. Be sure to check the seals on the jars the next day, to be sure that they remain tight before storing the jars in a cool, dry, and preferably dark location.

WATER-BATH CANNING

One way to avoid having to use a pressure canner is to can chiles along with high-acid vegetables or liquids. One example would be salsas. This will raise the acid level of the mixture to the point that makes it safe to use the water-bath method of canning. In essence, to use this method, it is necessary to add vinegar, lemon juice, or lime juice in order to raise the acid level. If the addition of these ingredients raises the acid level to unpalatable levels, the amount of vinegar or lemon juice can be reduced, but the product must then be either pressure canned or frozen.

Water-bath canning can be done in a special pot, or in any large metal container that is deep enough so that the water level will be at least 2 inches over the tops of the jars, and can boil freely. A rack of some kind in the pot is also necessary to keep the jars off the bottom of the pot during the vigorous boiling of processing.

After the salsa has been prepared, it must reach boiling stage before simmering it for 5 minutes. Pour it into hot, clean jars, being sure to use all the liquid, which is the high-acid portion of the salsa. Put on the lids and process in the water-bath for 30 minutes. Add boiling water during the process to keep the jars covered. When the processing time is finished, remove the jars to a draft-free location to cool.

The following tips apply to the water-bath method: equal parts of lemon or lime juice may be used to replace vinegar, if you so prefer. Less chile may be used in the salsas, but not more, since that will reduce the acid content of the final product. Additional salt may be safely added. Start timing the processing when the water starts to boil again, after adding the jars. And finally, additional seasonings such as oregano or cumin are best if added when serving the salsa, rather than before canning.

The New Mexico Department of Agriculture Cooperative Extension Service has shared the following recipes for canning chiles by the water-bath method.

GREEN CHILES AND TOMATOES

Before serving this cooked salsa, add 1 teaspoon cumin powder and stir in chopped cilantro. Serve as an all-purpose sauce with chips for a dip, with enchiladas or tacos, or as a relish or condiment with grilled meats, poultry, or fish.

- 3 cups peeled and chopped **Tomatoes**
- 3 cups chopped **New Mexico Green Chile**, roasted, peeled, seeds and stems removed (see Chapter 2 for roasting and peeling instructions)
- 1 1/2 teaspoons **Salt**
- 1 1/4 cups **White Vinegar**

Combine all of the ingredients in a saucepan, bring to a boil, cover, and simmer for 5 minutes.

Pack in hot, clean, sterilized jars, taking care to use all the liquid. Process in a hot water bath according to instructions on page 32.

Yield: 4 pints   *Heat Scale: Medium*

NEW MEXICO GREEN

PICANTE CHILE KETCHUP

Use this fiery version in place of regular catsup to spice up sandwiches, meatloaf, hot dogs, and hamburgers. It also tastes great in salad dressings and on french fries. If you wish, after puréeing, the ketchup may be frozen instead of canned.

6 pounds **Tomatoes**, peeled, seeded, and chopped
2 stalks **Celery**, chopped
1 large **Onion**, chopped
4 **Jalapeño** or **Serrano Chiles**, stems and seeds removed, chopped
    or substitute 2 **Habanero Chiles**
1 **Red Bell Pepper**, stem and seeds removed, chopped
1 cup **Brown Sugar**
1 1/2 cups **Cider Vinegar**
2 teaspoons **Dry Mustard**
1 teaspoon **Ground Cinnamon**
1/2 teaspoon **Ground Cloves**
1/4 teaspoon **Ground Allspice**
1 to 2 teaspoons **Salt**

In a pan on low heat, cook the tomatoes for 15 minutes, then drain off the juice. Add the celery, onion, chiles, and bell pepper and simmer for 1 hour.

Add the sugar, vinegar, and spices and simmer for an additional hour. Remove from the heat and purée until smooth.

Pour into hot, clean, sterilized jars and process in a hot water bath according to instruction on page 32.

Yield: 4 pints   *Heat Scale: Medium*

JALAPEÑO

A smallish, oval-shaped chile, it can vary in color from green to dark reddish-green to red. Red jalapeños are sweeter than green.

TACO SAUCE WITH GREEN CHILE

In addition to tacos, this simple sauce goes well with a variety of foods such as eggs and hamburgers. Before serving, try adding spices such as oregano, cinnamon, ground cloves, or cumin. For a hotter sauce, substitute jalapeños for the green chile.

3 cups chopped **New Mexico Green Chile**, roasted, peeled, stems and seeds removed (see Chapter 2 for roasting and peeling instructions)
3 cups peeled, chopped **Tomatoes**
3/4 cup chopped **Onion**
1 1/2 teaspoons **Salt**
3 cloves **Garlic**, minced
1 1/2 cups **Vinegar**

Combine all the ingredients in a pan, bring to a boil, cover, and simmer for 20 minutes.

Pack in hot, clean, sterilized jars, being sure to use all the liquid. Process according to the instructions on page 32.

Yield: 4 pints   *Heat Scale: Medium*

THE FOLLOWING RECIPES
CALL FOR CANNED GREEN CHILE:

CHILE CON QUESO SOUP

The classic combination of cheese and green chile appears here as a soup—rather than a dip or appetizer.

- 1 medium **Onion**, chopped
- 2 tablespoons **Butter** or **Margarine**
- 3 tablespoons **Flour**
- 3 to 4 cups **Chicken Broth**
- 1 cup chopped canned **Green Chile**
- 2 **Tomatoes**, peeled and chopped
- 1 **Bell Pepper**, stem and seeds removed, diced (optional)
- 1 1/2 cups **Half and Half**
- 8 ounces **Sharp Cheddar Cheese**, grated

In a sauce pot, sauté the onion in the butter until soft.

Add the flour to the pan and cook for 3 minutes, stirring constantly, taking care not to let the flour brown.

Stir in the broth, chile, tomatoes, bell pepper, and simmer for 30 minutes.

Bring to a boil, reduce the heat, add the half and half and the cheese and heat until the cheese melts and the soup is thickened.

Serves: 4 to 6   *Heat Scale: Hot*

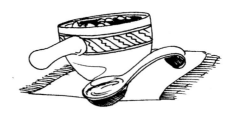

LOW-FAT HIGH-CHILE VICHYSSOISE

Of course, this version of the famous soup will be different from the heavily laden butter and cream recipes of the past. For one, it will have a lot more heat for a cold soup because we've replaced the fat with chile.

Note: This recipe requires advance preparation.

2 tablespoons **Olive Oil**
2 cups chopped **Leeks**
2 cups chopped **Onions**
1 1/2 quarts **Chicken Broth**
1/2 teaspoon **Habanero Powder**
1/4 cup chopped fresh **Basil**
4 **White Potatoes**, peeled and diced
1 cup canned chopped **New Mexico Green Chile**
1 cup **Evaporated Skim Milk**
1 cup **Non-Fat Sour Cream**
1 cup skim **Milk**
1 teaspoon **Ground White Pepper**
Freshly minced **Chives**
New Mexico Red Chile Powder

In a large soup pot, heat the olive oil and sauté the leeks and onions until soft, about 10 minutes. Add the broth, habanero powder, basil, potatoes, and green chile, and bring to a boil. Reduce the heat and simmer until the potatoes are tender, about 20 minutes.

Remove from the heat and purée in batches in a food processor until the mixture is a very smooth, thin paste. Transfer to a bowl and add the evaporated skim milk, non-fat sour cream, skim milk, and white pepper. Mix well, taste for heat, and add hot chile powder if too mild. Cover and refrigerate for at least 5 hours. Serve in cold bowls garnished with minced chives and a sprinkling of red chile powder.

Serves: 8   *Heat Scale: Mild to Medium*

New Mexico
Green Chile Salad

The versatility of canned green chile is demonstrated in this delicious salad.

Mixed Greens, such as **Romaine, Butter Lettuce**, or **Spinach**
1 **Hard-boiled Egg**, peeled and sliced
1/4 cup canned **Green Chile Strips**
1 **Chicken Breast** (boned and skinless), marinated in **Teriyaki Sauce**, grilled, and cut into 6 long, thin pieces
1/4 cup **Guacamole** (or 4 ripe **Avocado** slices)
2 tablespoons **Salsa** of choice
6 **Tostada Chips**
1/4 cup cooked **Garbanzo Beans**
2 tablespoons chopped **Green Onions**
2 tablespoons diced **Tomatoes**
Grated **Cheddar Cheese** for garnish

Place the greens on 2 plates and cover them with the hard-boiled egg slices. Place the chile strips and chicken strips alternately on top of the egg slices. To finish, scoop the guacamole on top, followed by the salsa on top of the guacamole. Crown each with 3 tostada chips stuck into the guacamole. Sprinkle the salad with the beans, onions, and tomatoes and garnish with the cheese.

Serves: 2   *Heat Scale: Mild*

GREEN CHILE SCONES

These tender and flaky scones are best served warm from the oven. For entertaining, try cutting the scones out with Southwestern cookie cutters such as a saguaro cactus, a chile, or a cowboy boot.

2 cups **All-Purpose Flour**
1 teaspoon **Salt**
1 tablespoon **Baking Powder**
1/3 cup chopped canned **Green Chile**
2 cloves **Garlic**, minced
1 cup plus 2 tablespoons **Whipping Cream**, divided

Preheat the oven to 425 degrees F.

In a bowl, mix together the flour, salt, and baking powder. Add the chile, garlic, and 1 cup of the cream and stir until a soft dough forms. Place the dough on a floured surface and knead 10 times or until the mixture forms a ball.

Divide the dough into two pieces. Pat each piece out to a 10-inch circle on an ungreased cookie sheet. Brush the top of each circle with the remaining cream.

Bake for 15 minutes or until golden brown. Cut each circle into 8 wedges before serving.

Yield: 16 scones   *Heat Scale: Mild*

SOUTHWEST SALSA SOUP WITH LIME CREAM

Using a prepared salsa as a base for this soup makes it quick and easy to prepare, as well as allowing you to choose your spice level, from mild to wild. The heat of the salsa will intensify, so we don't recommend you use a habanero-based salsa or any other that is too hot. This simple soup can also be made more hearty with the addition of cooked pinto or black beans, chicken or turkey, or even whole-kernel corn. Add these to the soup after it has been pureed. For the taste of green chile and chicken enchiladas in soup form, just use green chile salsa and add chicken.

2 to 3 teaspoons **Vegetable Oil**
1 cup chopped **Onion**
2 teaspoons chopped **Garlic**
1 1/2 cups tomato-based **Prepared Salsa with New Mexican Green Chile**
3 cups **Chicken Broth**, preferably homemade
2 **Corn Tortillas**, torn into pieces
1/4 teaspoon **Ground Cumin**
Salt and freshly **Ground Black Pepper** to taste
1/4 cup chopped, fresh **Cilantro**
Lime Cream (1/2 cup **Cream** mixed with two teaspoons of **Lime Juice**) for garnish

Heat a heavy saucepan or stockpot over medium-high heat, add the oil, and when hot, add the onions and sauté until they are soft. Add the garlic and continue to sauté for an additional minute.

Stir in the salsa, broth, tortillas, cumin, and salt and pepper and bring to a boil. Reduce the heat and simmer until the tortillas are soft. Remove from the heat and cool slightly.

Put the mixture into a blender or food processor and puree until smooth. Taste and adjust the seasonings and stir in the cilantro.

To serve, ladle the soup into individual bowls and garnish with a dollop of lime cream.

Yield: 4 to 6 servings

Heat scale: Varies according to the heat of the salsa

4. ICED HEAT: FREEZING CHILES

Freezing chiles is an excellent way of preserving them. Chiles that have been frozen retain all the characteristics of fresh chiles except for their texture. Since the individual cell walls have been ruptured by the freezing of the water within each cell, the chiles will lose their crisp texture.

Another result of the freezing process, according to one source, is the spread of capsaicin throughout the chile. This occurs with the rupturing of the cell walls and can actually make some chiles seem hotter after freezing than they were beforehand. Research to date indicates that freezing chiles does not make them hotter. There is simply nothing that the freezing process alone can do, either physically or chemically, to increase the heat of a chile.

There are different requirements for freezing chiles, depending on the size of the chile. Large chiles may be frozen at any stage once they have been roasted. (See Chapter 2 for instructions.) That is, they may be frozen before peeling (freezing actually makes them easier to peel), or after peeling and de-seeding. They may be frozen whole or chopped.

The easiest way to freeze large chiles is to put them into freezer bags, double-bag them to prevent freezer burn and place in the freezer. You can also wrap them in heavy foil or freezer wrap, or you can pack them in rigid plastic containers. A handy way to freeze chopped New Mexico green chile is in plastic ice cube trays. After the trays are frozen, the chile cubes can be popped out and stored in bags. The cubes can then be used when making soups or stews, or in other recipes, without having to pry apart blocks of frozen chiles. Mix chiles with a little water before putting in trays—the cubes freeze more solidly.

Smaller varieties, including habaneros, serranos, jalapeños, and Thai chiles can be frozen without processing. Just wash off the chiles and allow them to dry before freezing. Then place them on a cookie sheet or other flat surface, one layer deep, and put them in the freezer until frozen solid. They can then be stored in double freezer bags and will keep for 9 to 12 months at zero degrees F. Sometimes they

dry out a bit and need to be soaked in water during defrosting to rehydrate them.

Fresh red chile paste (see Chapter 2) can be stored in plastic containers or zip bags and frozen to use all year long. The paste holds up well in the freezer and really helps to cut meal preparation time.

FROZEN CHILE MASH

Here is one of the best methods for processing and preserving large quantities of small chile pods quickly. The method is so basic that it is sometimes overlooked among preservation methods. You should have a powerful blender or food processor for this. To use, defrost the cubes and estimate 2 to 3 pods per cube. Use in recipes calling for minced or chopped small chiles.

Fresh small **Chile Pods**, such as **Jalapeño, Habanero,** or **Rocoto,**
    stems and seeds removed
Water as needed

Place the chile pods in a food processor or blender with a little water and process to a medium-thin purée. Take care not to breathe the fumes from the puréeing. Pour the purée into plastic ice cube trays and freeze solid. Pop the cubes out and double bag them in zip bags. Label and place back in the freezer.

Yield: Varies   *Heat Scale: Hot to Extremely Hot*

TEXAS GREEN SAUCE

When you order "green sauce" in Texas, this is what you will be served. It differs from New Mexico's green sauce in that the color is derived from tomatillos rather than from green chiles. This sauce can be used as a dipping sauce, with enchiladas, or as a topping for grilled poultry or fish. It will keep for several weeks in the refrigerator.

3 pounds **Tomatillos**, husks removed
1 bunch **Green Onions**
1 small bunch **Cilantro**
1 tablespoon **Garlic** in oil
2 teaspoons **Sugar**
2 teaspoons **Lime Juice**
1 tablespoon **Chicken Base** dissolved in 2 tablespoons **Water**
6 frozen **Serrano Chiles**, defrosted and stems removed

Roast the tomatillos in a roasting pan under the broiler until they are brown and squishy. Turn them over with a pair of tongs and repeat the process. Take the roasted tomatillos, including all the liquid from the roasting process, and combine them with the remaining ingredients in a food processor and purée.

Simmer this mixture in a pot for ten minutes before serving or incorporating into another recipe.

Yield: 4 cups   *Heat Scale: Medium*

JALAPEÑOS & SERRANOS

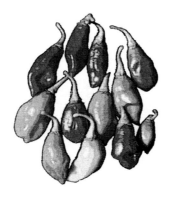

HABANERO MANGO MUSTARD SAUCE

This sauce from the eastern Caribbean is excellent over fried seafood. It will keep for 3 weeks in the refrigerator.

- 1/3 cup **Cider Vinegar**
- 1/4 cup **Hot Mustard Powder**
- 1 cup chopped **Onion**
- 2 teaspoons grated **Ginger**
- 2 tablespoons **Vegetable Oil**
- 1 15-ounce can **Mango**, drained
- 2 frozen **Habanero Chiles**, defrosted, stems and seeds removed, chopped

In a bowl, pour the vinegar over the mustard and let sit for 15 minutes.

In a pan, sauté the onion and ginger in oil until soft.

Place all the ingredients in a blender or food processor and purée until smooth.

Return to the pan and simmer the sauce for 5 minutes to blend the flavors.

Yield: 2 cups   *Heat Scale: Hot*

HABANEROS

COCONUT-CHILE CHUTNEY

This chutney from the southwest coast of India is served with curry dishes but also can be used as a dip with fried plantains. After using, place in a jar in the refrigerator; it keeps for at least three months.

1 tablespoon **Tamarind Pulp** (or two teaspoons **Lime Juice**)
2 cups shredded **Coconut**
1 1-inch piece **Ginger**, peeled
8 frozen **Jalapeño Chiles**, defrosted, stems and seeds removed, cut in half
4 cloves **Garlic**
1/2 cup **Cilantro**
6 large **Green Mangoes**, peeled and seeds removed
1 teaspoon **Cumin Seeds**
1 teaspoon **Fenugreek Seeds**
4 tablespoons **Olive** or **Vegetable Oil**
1/2 teaspoon **Mustard Seeds**
1 teaspoon **Red Chile Powder**
1 teaspoon **Turmeric Powder**
1/2 cup **Cilantro Leaves**
Salt to taste

Soak the tamarind in 1/2 cup warm water for 10 minutes, then strain the pulp and save the liquid.

In a food processor, grind coconut, ginger, chiles, garlic, and cilantro into a fine paste. In a bowl, combine the paste with the tamarind water and set aside.

Place the mangoes in a blender or food processor along with the cumin and fenugreek and process into a smooth paste.

Heat the oil in a large skillet over medium heat for 1 minute. Reduce the heat and add the mustard seeds. When the seeds begin to pop, add the mango paste, chile powder, turmeric, and coconut-tamarind paste. Add a little water, mix well, and cook over low heat for 10 minutes, stirring occasionally.

Remove from the heat and add the cilantro and salt. Allow to cool to room temperature before serving.

Yield: 4 to 6 cups   *Heat Scale: Medium*

GREEN CHILE STEW BORDER-STYLE

This enormously popular dish is sometimes called caldillo, *or "little broth" in Spanish. There are probably as many versions of this stew as there are cooks in the Southwest.*

2 pounds **Pork Stew Meat,** cut into 1-inch cubes
2 tablespoons **Vegetable Oil**
1 large **Onion**, chopped
1 teaspoon chopped **Garlic**
2 cups frozen chopped **New Mexico Green Chile**
2 large **Tomatoes**, peeled and chopped
2 **Potatoes**, peeled and diced
1/2 teaspoon **Ground Cumin**
3 cups **Chicken** or **Beef Broth**
Salt to taste

In a saucepan, brown the pork in the oil. Add the onions and garlic and sauté until the onion is soft. Remove the meat and onion mixture from the pan. Add 1 cup water to deglaze the pan.

Combine the pan drippings and the rest of the ingredients in a large pot or Dutch oven, bring to a boil, reduce the heat, and simmer for 2 hours, or until the meat is very tender and starts to fall apart.

Serves: 6   *Heat Scale: Medium*

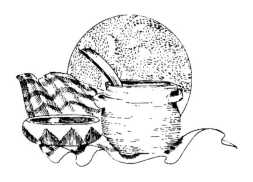

Spicy Gazpacho

(Andalusian Cold Tomato Soup)

Gazpacho *was originally a simple peasant dish, consisting only of bread, garlic, salt, vinegar, oil, and water. After the discovery of the New World, tomatoes and peppers were also included. The following recipe is for classic tomato-based* gazpacho, *the best known version of this soup. But the Spaniards have dozens of soups called* gazpacho—*cold or hot; thick or thin; red, white, green, or yellow-made from a wide range of ingredients. Serve the chilled* gazpacho *in individual soup bowls and pass around small bowls of various garnishes to sprinkle on top of the* gazpacho, *according to the diner's choice.*

Note: This recipe requires advance preparation.

1 cup frozen chopped **New Mexico Green Chile**
1 **Green Bell Pepper**, seeded and deveined, coarsely chopped
1 **Red Bell Pepper**, seeded and deveined, coarsely chopped
6 medium-sized ripe **Tomatoes**, preferably fresh; if not, use canned
   Tomatoes and their **Juice** in place of the **Tomato Juice** (*)
1 large **Onion**
2 medium **Cucumbers**, peeled
3 cloves **Garlic**
1 cup coarsely crumbled, crustless **French Bread**
2 tablespoons **Tomato** paste
3 cups **Tomato Juice***
6 tablespoons **Olive Oil**
1/4 cup **Red Wine Vinegar**
1 tablespoon mild **Spanish Paprika**
1 to 2 teaspoons **Salt**
1/8 teaspoon **Cumin**
Bottled Hot Sauce to taste

Garnishes:

1/2 cup chopped **Onion** or **Spring Onions** sliced into thin rings
1/2 cup each chopped **Green, Red,** and **Yellow Bell Peppers**
1/2 cup peeled and chopped **Cucumber**
1/4 cup chopped **Chives**
1 to 2 cups **Fried Croutons**

Purée the green chile, bell peppers, tomatoes, onion, cucumbers, garlic, and bread together in a food processor or blender. (Process the ingredients in batches, if necessary.) Transfer the puréed ingredients to a large bowl. Dissolve the tomato paste in the tomato juice, add to the puréed ingredients, and mix well. Whisk in the olive oil, wine vinegar, paprika, salt, and cumin, until all ingredients are thoroughly combined. Cover and refrigerate for several hours before serving. Serve cold, add hot sauce to taste, and use several garnishes (at least four is recommended).

Serves: 8 to 10   *Heat Scale: Varies*

CHILE RAJAS CON QUESO

Rajas are strips of roasted and peeled chiles of any kind, but usually New Mexico or problanos. This appetizer is a spin on traditional chile con queso dip.

3 frozen **New Mexico Green Roasted Chile Pods**, defrosted; stems removed, peeled, seeded, and cut into strips
2 **Serrano Chiles**, stems removed, seeded, and diced
2 tablespoons **Butter**
2 cloves **Garlic**, diced
1/2 cup diced **Onions**
1/2 cup diced fresh **Tomatoes**
1/3 cup minced fresh **Cilantro**
1 cup shredded **Monterey Jack Cheese**
1 tablespoon **Sour Cream**

In a pan, sauté all of the ingredients except the cheese and sour cream in the butter for 2 to 3 minutes. Sprinkle the cheese on top, cover, and cook over low heat for 30 seconds. Remove from the heat and allow to set for 1 minute.

Pour the mixture into a bowl and top with the sour cream. Serve with fresh tostada chips for dipping.

Serves: 4   *Heat Scale: Medium*

CALABACITAS CON CHILES VERDES

(SQUASH WITH GREEN CHILES)

Squash and corn are familiar accompaniments throughout the Southwest. This side dish is particularly good with traditional entrées such as enchiladas, tamales, and burritos.

1 cup chopped **Onions**
2 cloves **Garlic**, minced
1 tablespoon **Bacon Drippings** or **Vegetable Oil**
1/2 cup frozen chopped **New Mexico Green Chile**
2 medium **Zucchinis**, thinly sliced
1 cup **Whole Kernel Corn**
1/3 cup **Cream** or **Half and Half**

In a pan, sauté the onions and garlic in the drippings until soft.

Add the chiles, zucchinis, and corn. Simmer for 5 minutes or until the squash is almost done.

Add the cream, increase the heat until the cream starts to boil and cook until the vegetables are done and the sauce has thickened.

Serves: 6   *Heat Scale: Medium*

RED CHILE RISTRA

CHRISTINE'S HOT SAUCE

I confess I've never met Christine. Her recipe was passed on to us by friends in Scottsdale, and it's a good example of an Arizona-style, all-purpose hot sauce that can be used for a chip dip or can be added to soups and stews.

2 tablespoons **Chiltepins**
1 cup frozen **New Mexican Fresh Red Chile**, thawed
1 1/2 cloves **Garlic**
1/2 **Onion**, minced
1/4 teaspoon **Cumin**
Pinch of **Oregano**
Pinch of **Salt**
2 tablespoons **Vegetable Oil**
2 tablespoons **Vinegar**
8-ounce can **Tomato Sauce**

Puree all ingredients, except the tomato sauce, in a blender, then place the mixture in a bowl. Add the tomato sauce and mix well.

Yield: 2 cups   *Heat Scale: Hot*

CHILE CON CARNE WITH FROZEN RED OR GREEN CHILE

Here is a classic recipe from Nancy, who commented: "When you order 'chili' in New Mexico, this is what you will be served. It is a basic recipe that has its roots in very old Pueblo Indian cooking. Beef can also be substituted in this recipe."

2 pounds **Pork**, cut into 3/4-inch cubes
2 tablespoons **Vegetable Oil**
3 cloves **Garlic**, minced
2 cups frozen **New Mexican Chile**, fresh red or green, thawed
3 cups **Water** or **Beef Broth**
Salt to taste

Brown the pork in the oil in a Dutch oven. Add the garlic and saute. Pour off any excess fat. Add the chile, pork and water, bring to a boil, reduce the heat and simmer, covered, until the pork is very tender and starts to fall apart, at least 2 hours.

Yield: 6-8 servings   *Heat Scale: Medium*

5 PODS TO POWDER

The oldest, easiest, and most common way to preserve chiles is to dry them. Aside from a few of the thick-walled, meaty varieties such as jalapeños, most chiles are well-preserved by drying them at home. There are several different ways to dry chiles, employing both traditional methods and new technologies.

MAKING RISTRAS

The ristra, or chile string, is the oldest and also the most attractive drying method, and there are several different ways of assembling these strings. Traditional ristras are made by tying New Mexico red chiles together in clusters of three, with cotton string. Start by wrapping the string around the three stems a couple of times, then bring the string up between two of the chiles, and finish off with a half-hitch over the stems. Continue using the same piece of string, tying up groups of three chiles until it gets too awkward to handle. Just cut the string and start again. To make a 36" ristra will require around 15 pounds of fresh red pods.

When all the chiles have been strung by threes, they then get braided onto a length of strong twine or wire. Hanging the twine from an overhead support greatly simplifies this stage of assembly. Braid the chiles from the bottom of the twine as if braiding hair, using the twine as one braid and chiles from each grouping as the other two. Be sure to push each group down tightly against each other to ensure an attractive, full-bodied ristra.

These days, some ristra makers have resorted to using rubber bands to "tie" up the groups of three chiles, then slipping each group over a wire to form the ristra. This method is considerably faster than the traditional method; the downside is that the ristras tend to be a bit thin or skinny and last only as long as the rubber bands hold out.

One final method to make a ristra is to use a large needle threaded with string. Push the needle through the bottom of the stem where it widens out, pushing the chiles up tightly against each other. Again this tends to produce thin looking ristras, but this can be overcome by hanging several strings together. It is also a handy way to handle smaller chiles such as cayennes or piquíns, which require a lot of time and dexterity to string in the traditional way.

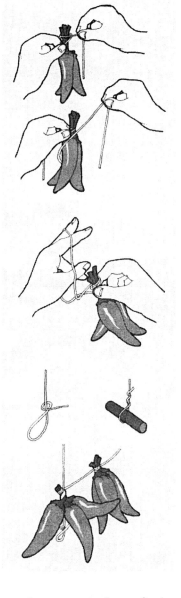

Unless you live in an arid climate, it is important to dry your ristras in a location where the air circulates freely. If hung inside a home in a damp climate, there is a good chance that some of the chiles will rot. Hung from a tree, or in an open porch should give the ristra a good chance to dry properly. If a few of the chiles do start to rot, just pull them off the string; if you've got a nice full ristra, you'll never miss them!

Another good reason to dry your ristra outside is that if any of the chiles start to rot, they may start dripping a liquid that will stain anything it touches. (After all, red chiles are used to produce red coloring that is used in food products.) So you might want to reconsider before hanging your fresh ristra over your 2-inch deep, snow white pile carpet. And one final disturbing note: chiles that turn bad attract fruit flies by the zillions. Obviously, it makes a lot of sense to hang them outside to dry!

OTHER DRYING METHODS

Another way to dry chiles, and in fact, nearly the only way to dry some of the thick-fleshed chiles, is to use a food dehydrator. As we mentioned earlier, jalapeños and several other chiles simply will not air dry. They will, however, dry well in a dehydrator. Simply place them in a single layer on the racks and follow the instructions for your model. Cutting the thick fleshed chiles in half, or into several pieces helps to speed up the process.

Many people think that drying in an oven is just as effective, which unfortunately, is not always the case. Dehydrators supply not only heat, they also constantly circulate air through the unit. Ovens usually supply only heat, which means that meaty chiles could possibly spoil, rather than dry.

If you do use an oven, use the lowest possible heat. Cut the chiles in half, remove the seeds, and place on a baking tray. Check the chiles every hour or so to make sure they are not burning. When they are brittle, they are ready.

It's possible to dry chiles in a microwave oven. By chopping the chiles into small pieces and microwaving them in small quantities, chiles can be dried in no time at all, especially the smaller, thin-fleshed varieties. However, this method will not work for whole pods.

Roasted and peeled fresh green New Mexico chiles can also be dried, and, in fact, drying fresh green was the only way to preserve it in the days before freezers. See the recipe which follows. A word of warning: don't get upset by the appearance of the dried green since it turns black and looks more like road-kill than anything you'd want to eat! However, when rehydrated, it plumps up, turns almost green, and is extremely tasty.

MAKING POWDERS

All dried chiles can be ground into powder—and most are, including the habanero. Crushed chiles, or those coarsely ground with some of the seeds are called *quebrado.* Coarse powders are referred to as *caribe,* while the finer powders are termed *molido.* The milder powders, such as New Mexico chile powder, can also be used as the

base for sauces, but the hotter powders such as cayenne and piquín are used when heat is needed more than flavor.

Adventurous cooks can experiment with creating powders of specific colors. For example, collect the different varieties of green, yellow, orange, red, and brown chiles and separate them into their respective colors. The colors of the powders vary from a bright, electric red-orange (chiltepins), to light green (dried jalapeños), to a dark brown that verges on black (ancho). The colored powders can then be combined with spices, as in our recipe for Chili Powder (this chapter), or they can be stored for later use. Another use for the powders is to turn them into green, yellow, orange, red, or brown chile pastes. Since some of the colors of the powders tend to be a bit dull, they can be brightened up by adding a few drops of the appropriate food coloring when making the pastes.

In some kitchens, there are more powders available than the whole pods because the powders are concentrated and take up less storage space. Store the powders in small, airtight glass bottles. The fresher the powders, the better they taste, so don't grind up too many pods. Use an electric spice mill and be sure to wear a painter's mask to protect your nose and throat from the pungent powder. Many cooks experiment by changing the powders called for in recipes.

CHILE PASADO

(CHILE OF THE PAST)

Here is the way green chile was preserved before the invention of canning and freezers. This method assumes that you live in a dry climate like New Mexico or Arizona. If not, remove the stems from the chile and place the pods in a food dehydrator until brittle. You can place them in an oven set at the lowest heat possible, but you must monitor them carefully. There are about 10 medium-sized pods to a pound.

2 pounds **New Mexico Green Chile Pods** (about 20 **Pods**)
String

Roast the chile pods on a charcoal or gas grill until the pods blister and start to turn black, turning often. Remove them from the grill and place in a plastic bag with a wet paper towel for 1/2 hour.

Remove and carefully peel the skin off, leaving the stem and seeds intact. Tie four pods together by wrapping string around the stems and place over a line outside in the sun. Do not let the chiles get wet by rain, and you can protect them from flies and other insects by wrapping them lightly in cheesecloth. Drying time varies with humidity levels, but dry them until they are very dark and brittle. To store, break off the stems and place the dried pods in a zip bag and then place in a second zip bag. Place in the freezer for optimum results, especially if you live in a humid climate. Because they are brittle, breaking off the stems will sometimes cause the pods to break into strips and other pieces.

To reconstitute the pods, place them in a pot of boiling water for 1 minute. Remove from the heat and let stand for five minutes. Remove from the water and drain. Use them in any recipe calling for green chile in any form, except whole pods.

Yield: About 3 ounces   *Heat Scale: Varies but usually medium*

ANCHO CHILE DRY RUB

Here's great rub to use on meats that will be smoked or grilled. Since anchos are sold in fairly pliable condition, place them in the oven on low heat until they are brittle.

4 **Ancho Chiles**, stems and seeds removed, dried in the oven
2 teaspoons **Whole White Peppercorns**
1 teaspoon **Whole Black Peppercorns**
1/2 teaspoon **Celery Seed**
3 1/2 teaspoons **Cumin Seed**
1 teaspoon **Thyme**
1 small **Bay Leaf**
1 teaspoon **Annato Powder**
1 1/2 teaspoons **Salt**

Blend together all the ingredients in a spice mill or blender. Pack in a glass jar after using.

Yield: About 1/2 cup   *Heat Scale: Mild*

CAJUN RUB

Here's a concentrated rub that has its origins in Louisiana, where it seems that every home cook has his or her own secret spice mixture for grilled foods. This rub works well on fish and is especially good on shrimp. Sprinkle it on the seafood and allow it to marinate at room temperature for about an hour. This rub is also good on chicken before it's grilled.

1 tablespoon **Paprika**

5 cayenne **Pods**, stems and seeds removed, ground into **Powder**

2 teaspoons **Garlic Powder**

1 teaspoon freshly ground **Black Pepper**

1 teaspoon dried **Thyme**

1 teaspoon dried **Oregano**

1 teaspoon **Onion Powder**

1 teaspoon **Salt**

1 **Bay Leaf**, center stem removed, crushed

1/2 teaspoon **Ground Allspice**

1/4 teaspoon **Ground White Pepper**

Combine all the ingredients in a spice grinder and process until finely ground. Store any unused rub in a sealed container in the freezer.

Yield: 2 1/2 tablespoons　　　　　　　　　*Heat Scale: Medium*

SOUTH-OF-THE-BORDER CHILE RUB

This is our version of Mexican flavorings that would work on goat, as in cabrito (pit roasted goat). Can't find goat at the supermarket? Use this rub for grilling or smoking beef, pork, and lamb.

- 3 tablespoons ground **Ancho Chile**
- 2 teaspoons ground **Chile de Arbol**
- 2 teaspoons ground **Chipotle Chile**
- 2 teaspoons dried **Oregano**, Mexican preferred
- 2 teaspoons **Onion Salt**
- 1 teaspoon **Ground Cumin**
- 1 teaspoon powdered **Garlic**

Combine all the ingredients in a bowl and mix well. Store any unused rub in a sealed container in the freezer.

Yield: Approximately 2/3 cup   *Heat Scale: Hot*

CHILI POWDER

This powder is used to make chili con carne and replaces the commercial type; experiment with the ingredients and adjust them to your taste.

- 5 tablespoons ground **New Mexico Red Chile**
- 1 tablespoon ground **Hot Chile**, such as **Piquín** or **Chiltepin**
- 1 1/2 tablespoons **Ground Cumin**
- 1 1/2 tablespoons ground **Oregano**
- 1 1/2 tablespoons **Garlic Powder**
- 1 teaspoon **Salt**

Mix all the ingredients together and process in a blender or spice grinder until fine. Store the excess powder in a glass jar.

Yield: 1/2 cup   *Heat Scale: Hot*

DRY JERK SEASONING

Jerk seasoning is actually a delicious, tropical way to barbecue. Use it to season either pork or poultry; simply rub into the meat, marinate overnight in the refrigerator, grill or bake, and then enjoy!

1 teaspoon dried ground **Habanero Chile** or substitute other hot powder such as cayenne
2 tablespoons **Onion Powder**
2 teaspoons ground **Thyme**
2 teaspoons **Ground Allspice**
1 teaspoon coarsely ground **Black Pepper**
1/2 teaspoon **Ground Nutmeg**
1/2 teaspoon **Ground Cinnamon**
1/2 teaspoon **Garlic Powder**
1/4 teaspoon **Ground Cloves**

Combine all the ingredients and mix well. Store the seasoning in a glass jar.

Yield: About 1/4 cup   *Heat Scale: Hot*

HABANERO

A distinctively flavored, extremely hot chile. Small and lantern-shaped, it is native to the Caribbean, the Yucatan and the north coast of South America. Habaneros range from bright orange to red when ripe.

CURRY POWDER

Curry powder is always a combination of various ingredients, and much like chili con carne, there is no such thing as a definitive recipe. There are instead as many curry recipe as there are curry cooks. Use this recipe as a starting point and make additions or adjustments according to your tastes. Homemade curry powder is a wonderful treat for your taste buds.

5 tablespoons ground **New Mexico Red Chile**
3 tablespoons **Ground Coriander**
3 tablespoons **Ground Cumin**
1 tablespoon **Ground Ginger**
2 teaspoons **Ground Cayenne**
1 teaspoon **Cardamom Seeds**
1 teaspoon **Ground Fenugreek**
1 teaspoon freshly ground **Black Pepper**
1 teaspoon **Ground Allspice**
1 teaspoon **Ground Cloves**
1/2 teaspoon **Ground Nutmeg**

Mix all the ingredients together and process in a blender or spice grinder until fine. Store the powder in a glass jar.

Yield: 1 1/2 cups   *Heat Scale: Mild*

RED CHILE SAUCE FROM PODS

This basic sauce can be used in a variety of Southwestern dishes that call for a red sauce, as well as in place of ketchup when making salad dressings and other dishes. Other large dried chiles such as guajillo, pasilla, or ancho chiles can be added or substituted. This sauce will keep up to one week in the refrigerator, or you can freeze it.

12 dried whole **New Mexico Red Chiles**
1 large **Onion**, chopped
3 cloves **Garlic**, chopped
3 cups **Chicken Broth** or **Water**

Place the chiles on a baking pan and put in a 250 degree F oven for 10 to 15 minutes or until the chiles smell like they are toasted, being careful not to let them burn. Remove the stems and seeds and crumble the pods into a saucepan.

Add the remaining ingredients, bring to a boil, reduce the heat, and simmer for 20 to 30 minutes or until the chiles are soft.

Purée the mixture in a blender or a food processor until smooth and strain. If the sauce is too thin, place it back on the stove and simmer until it is reduced to the desired consistency.

Yield: 2 to 2 1/2 cups   *Heat Scale: Medium*

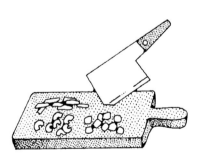

RED CHILE SAUCE FROM POWDER

This is a basic recipe that can be used interchangeably with any of the mild red chile powders. (If this sauce were made from some of the hotter powders such as piquín, it would be too hot to eat!) Adjust the amount of powder to change the pungency of the sauce.

2 tablespoons **Vegetable Oil**
1 medium **Onion**, chopped
2 cloves **Garlic**, minced
2 tablespoons **All-Purpose Flour**
3 to 4 tablespoons **New Mexico Red Chile Powder**
1/4 teaspoon **Ground Cumin** (optional)
3 cups **Chicken Broth** or **Water**
Salt to taste

In a pan, heat the oil and sauté the onion and garlic until they are slightly browned. Add the flour and continue to cook for 4 minutes, stirring constantly, until the flour is browned, being careful that it does not burn.

Stir in the chile powder and cumin and heat for a couple of minutes.

Add the broth, bring to a boil, reduce the heat, and simmer for 10 to 15 minutes or until the desired consistency is obtained. Salt to taste.

Variation: For a smoother sauce, either purée the onion and garlic or substitute 1 teaspoon onion powder and 1/8 teaspoon garlic powder and add along with the chile powder.

Yield: 2 cups   *Heat Scale: Medium*

W.C.'S CHIMAYÓ RED CHILE SAUCE

Even in the heart of chileland in Albuquerque, our friend W.C. Longacre is famous for this red chile sauce that is served over burritos and other New Mexican entrées. The key is a rich, high-impact chicken stock that is made in the style of classic French poaching stocks, with plenty of herbs. W.C. uses Chimayó chile in this recipe, a flavorful variety from northern New Mexico that has a brilliant red-orange color. Divide this into 2-cup servings and freeze in zip bags.

1/4 cup **Vegetable Oil**
5 cloves **Garlic**
1 medium **Onion**, chopped
1 1/2 teaspoons **Thyme**
1/3 ounce **Baker's Unsweetened Chocolate**, coarsely chopped
1 tablespoon **Salt**
1 1/2 pounds ground **New Mexico Red Chile**, Chimayó preferred
1 gallon homemade **Chicken Stock** or substitute broth

In a blender or food processor, combine the oil, garlic, onion, thyme, chocolate, salt, and purée to a coarse paste. Transfer to a bowl, add the ground red chile and mix.

In a large pot, heat the chicken broth to boiling. Add the paste and boil for 10 minutes, stirring occasionally. Add approximately 1 quart of water and boil for 5 minutes, or longer, until reaching the desired consistency, stirring constantly.

Yield: About 1 gallon   *Heat Scale: Medium*

Salsa Casera

(Chiltepin House Sauce)

This diabolically hot sauce is also called chiltepin pasta (paste). It's a great way to preserve a bountiful harvest of chiltepins or chile piquins. Use it in soups and stews and to fire up machaca, eggs, tacos, tostadas, and beans. This is the exact recipe prepared in the home of Josefina Duran in Cumpas, Sonora, and it keeps in the refrigerator for months. It can also be used like a mash as a basis for other hot sauces.

- 2 cups **Dried Chiltepins**
- 8 to 10 cloves **Garlic**
- 1 teaspoon **Salt**
- 1 teaspoon dried **Oregano**, Mexican preferred
- 1 teaspoon **Coriander Seed**
- 1 cup **Cider Vinegar**

Combine all of the ingredients along with 1 cup water in a blender or food processor and purée on high speed for 3 to 4 minutes. For the best results, refrigerate for one day to blend the flavors. It keeps indefinitely in the refrigerator.

Yield: 2 cups   *Heat Scale: Extremely hot*

HARISSA SAUCE

This classic sauce is thought to be of Tunisian origin, but it is found throughout all of North Africa. It is used to flavor couscous and grilled dishes such as kebabs. Harissa Sauce reflects the region's love of spicy combinations, all with a definite cumin and coriander flavor. Cover this sauce with a thin film of olive oil, and it will keep up to a couple of months in the refrigerator.

10 dried whole **New Mexico Red Chiles**, stems and seeds removed
2 tablespoons **Olive Oil**
5 cloves **Garlic**
1 teaspoon **Ground Cumin**
1 teaspoon **Ground Cinnamon**
1 teaspoon **Ground Coriander**
1 teaspoon **Ground Caraway**

Cover the chiles with hot water and let them sit for 30 minutes until they soften. Remove and drain.

Place the chiles and remaining ingredients in a blender and purée until smooth using the chile water to thin it. The sauce should have the consistency of a thick paste.

Yield: 1 1/2 cups   *Heat Scale: Medium*

BERBERE PASTE

Berbere is the famous, or should we say, infamous, scorching Ethiopian hot sauce. One recipe we ran across called for over a cup of powdered cayenne! It is used as an ingredient in a number of dishes, a coating when drying meats, and as a side dish or condiment. Tribal custom dictated that it be served with kitfo, raw meat dishes, which we do not recommend. This sauce will keep for a couple of months under refrigeration. Serve sparingly as a condiment with grilled meats and poultry or add to soups and stews.

4 whole **Cardamom Pods**
2 teaspoons **Cumin Seeds**
1/2 teaspoon **Black Peppercorns**
1/2 teaspoon **Fenugreek Seeds**
1 small **Onion**, coarsely chopped
4 cloves **Garlic**
15 dried **Piquín Chiles**, stems removed
1 tablespoon **Ground Cayenne**
2 tablespoons **Ground Paprika**
1/2 teaspoon **Ground Ginger**
1/4 teaspoon **Ground Allspice**
1/4 teaspoon **Ground Nutmeg**
1/4 teaspoon **Ground Cloves**
3 tablespoons **Vegetable Oil**

Toast the cardamom, cumin, peppercorns, and fenugreek in a hot skillet, shaking constantly, for a couple of minutes, until they start to crackle and "pop." In a spice mill, grind these spices to form a powder and set aside.

Combine the onion, garlic, and 1/2 cup water in a blender and purée until smooth. Add the chiles, cayenne, paprika, the ground spice mixture, ginger, allspice, nutmeg and cloves and continue to blend. Slowly add additional water and the oil and blend until smooth.

Remove to a saucepan and simmer the sauce for 15 minutes to blend the flavors and thicken.

Yield: About 1 cup   *Heat Scale: Extremely Hot*

ROASTED CORN
AND CRAB BISQUE

Roasting the corn gives this soup a distinctive flavor; the addition of crab is a Gulf Coast influence. Serve this bisque as the first course of a special holiday dinner.

3 ears of **Corn** with the husks left on
1 teaspoon crushed **Piquín** or other small hot dried **Red Chile**
1/4 cup diced **Bell Pepper**
1/2 cup chopped **Green Onions**
1 clove **Garlic**, minced
2 tablespoons **Butter** or **Vegetable Oil**
1 small **Potato**, peeled and diced
2 cups **Chicken Broth**
1/2 cup **White Wine**
1 cup **Milk**
1/2 cup **Cream** or **Half and Half**
1/2 pound **Lump Crab Meat**
Crushed **New Mexico Red Chile** for garnish

Soak the ears of corn, in their husks, in water for 30 minutes. Roast them by placing the ears on a hot grill and turning often until the corn is tender. Or, place them in a 400 degree F oven and roast them for 20 minutes. Cut the corn off the cobs.

Sauté the chile piquín, bell pepper, onions, and garlic in the butter until the onions are soft.

Combine the onion mixture, potato and broth in a pot and simmer for 30 minutes or until the potato is done. Add the wine, corn, and milk and simmer for 15 minutes. Stir in the cream and heat through.

Gently stir in the crab, taking care that the meat does not break down. Simmer for 3 minutes or until the crab is hot. Garnish with the crushed red chile and serve.

Serves: 4 to 6   *Heat Scale: Mild*

SANTA FE SALAD WITH CHILE PASADO DRESSING

If piñon nuts are not available, substitute sunflower seeds or chopped walnuts in this spicy tossed green salad.

THE DRESSING:

1/2 ounce **Chile Pasado**, reconstituted to make about 1/2 cup, chopped
1/4 cup **Mayonnaise**
2 tablespoons **Sour Cream**
1 tablespoon **Olive Oil**
1 tablespoon **Lime Juice**
1 clove **Garlic**, minced
1/4 teaspoon **Sugar**
1 teaspoon chopped fresh **Cilantro**
1/4 teaspoon **Ground Cumin**

Combine all the ingredients in a bowl and allow the dressing to sit for a few hours covered, in the refrigerator, to blend the flavors.

THE SALAD:

1/2 cup **Jicama**, diced, or substitute green apples
4 **Green Onions**, chopped, including the green part
2 **Red Ripe Tomatoes**, chopped
Mixed Salad Greens—Radicchio, Butter, and Red Leaf Lettuce
1/4 cup **Piñon Nuts**

Combine the jicama, onions, tomatoes, and salad greens. Toss with the dressing, top with the nuts, and serve.

Serves: 4 to 6   *Heat Scale: Medium*

SOUTHWESTERN JICAMA AND ORANGE SALAD

This spicy salad dressing goes well with a number of fruits and vegetables, so experiment with your own combinations.

THE DRESSING:

1 tablespoon crushed **Red Chile** or 1 teaspoon ground such as **New Mexico Red** or de arbol
2 tablespoons **Orange Juice**
1 tablespoon **Lime Juice**
1 tablespoon **White Vinegar**
1 teaspoon **Sugar**
1 clove **Garlic**, minced
1/2 teaspoon **Salt**
1/2 cup **Vegetable Oil**

Combine all the ingredients for the dressing except the oil and allow to sit for 30 minutes to blend the flavors. Whisk in the oil in a slow stream and mix until creamy.

THE SALAD:

1 small **Jicama**, peeled and diced
2 small **Orange**s, peeled and sectioned
1 small **Red Onion**, thinly sliced and separated into rings
Lettuce **Leaves**
Pine Nuts for garnish

Arrange the salad ingredients on a bed of lettuce. Pour the dressing over, top with the nuts, and serve.

Yield: 4 to 6 servings   *Heat Scale: Mild*

CAMARONES AL MOJO DE AJO
(SHRIMP IN GARLIC SAUCE)

This garlic shrimp dish hails from Guerrero, Mexico, but is commonly served in Mexican seafood restaurants in the Southwest. The shrimp are messy to peel and eat, but they are delicious.

2 tablespoons ground **New Mexico Red Chile**
10 cloves **Garlic**, crushed
Salt to taste
Freshly ground **Black Pepper** to taste
1 teaspoon **Vinegar**
24 large **Shrimp**, unpeeled
2 tablespoons **Olive Oil**
4 tablespoons **Butter**
2 tablespoons fresh **Lime Juice**

Crush together the chile, garlic, salt, pepper, and vinegar in a *molcaljete,* or mortar, and marinate the shrimp in half of the mixture for 1 hour.

Heat the oil and butter in a skillet, add the remaining garlic marinade, and sauté for 3 minutes. Add the shrimp and sauté another 3 minutes, turning often. Sprinkle the shrimp with lime juice and serve.

Serves: 4   *Heat Scale: Medium*

SOUTHWEST SEASONING RUB

This all-purpose rub adds a taste of the Southwest to whatever you use it on. It's a great grill rub for chicken, beef, and pork. It adds another chile dimension to salsas, and the chipotle's hint of smoke complements a pot of pinto beans.

2 tablespoons ground **Red New Mexico Chile**, such as Chimayó
2 teaspoons ground **Chile de Arbol**
1 teaspoon ground **Chipotle Chile**
2 teaspoon ground **Cumin**
1 teaspoon freshly ground **Black Pepper**
1 teaspoon **Garlic Salt**
1 teaspoon **Salt**

Combine all the ingredients in a bowl and stir to blend. Store the mixture in an airtight container.

Yield: 1/3 cup   *Heat scale: Medium*

SMOKED PRIME RIBS OF BEEF

Beef is smoked everywhere in the U.S. but the only area claiming it as the main barbecue meat is Texas—and that's mostly brisket and skirt steak. But we love barvecue prime rib especially. Buy a large prime rib roast and cut away the center. Then slice the ribless roast into ribeye steaks to use in other meals. Then slice the ribs apart so that more smoke will reach them. Serve these ribs with grilled potato wedges, a roasted corn salad, and buttermilk biscuits. Note: This recipe requires advance preparation.

8 large **Prime Ribs**
2/3 cup **South of the Border Chile Rub**, p. 00, or other rub of choosing
Chipotle Barbecue Sauce, p. 00, or other barbecue of choosing

Trim the excess fat off the ribs. Cover with the rub and massage the rub into the meat. Cover and let stand at room temperature for 1 hour.

Build a fire in the smoker and bring the smoke to 200 to 220 degrees F. Place the ribs on the grill or on racks and smoke for 4 1/2 hours, turning occasionally. One half hour before you remove the ribs from the smoker, brush the ribs all over with barbecue sauce.

Yield: 2-4 servings   *Heat Scale: Medium*

6 SMOKED CHILES

Why did Native Americans smoke chiles in the first place? Perhaps some thick-fleshed chiles such as early jalapeños were dropped near the communal fire and later, a leathery, preserved chile was the result. Since smoking is believed (along with salting) to be one of the earliest preservation methods, it would make sense that the "meaty" chiles could be smoked right along with the meat.

COMMERCIAL SMOKING

In the town of Delicias in northern Mexico, red jalapeños are smoked in a large pit on a rack that can be made out of wood, bamboo, or metal. Another nearby pit contains the fire and is connected to the smoking pit by an underground tunnel. The pods are placed on top of the rack where drafts of air pull the smoke up and over the pods. A farm may have a smoker of a different design at the edge of the fields, and it may be a fireplace of bricks with grates at the top and a firebox below. This smoker is for small batches.

HOME SMOKING

Chipotles smoked in the Mexican manner are not always available north of Mexico. And with prices of chipotles topping $15.00 per pound when they are available, an attractive alternative is for cooks to smoke their own chiles. As chile expert Paul Bosland of New Mexico State University commented, "It is possible to make chipotles in the backyard with a meat smoker or Weber-type barbecue with a lid. The grill should be washed to remove any meat particles because any odor in the barbecue will give the chile an undesirable flavor. Ideally, the smoker or barbecue should be new and dedicated only to smoking chiles." The result of this type of smoking is a chipotle that more resembles the red morita than the classic tan-brown típico.

There are five keys to the quality of the homemade chipotles: the maturity and quality of the pods, the moisture in the pods, the type of wood used to create the smoke, the temperature of the smoke drying the pods, and the amount of time the fruits are exposed to the smoke and heat. But remember that smoking is an art, so variations are to be expected and even desired.

Recommended woods are fruit trees or other hardwoods such as hickory, oak, and pecan. Pecan is used extensively in parts of Mexico and in southern New Mexico to flavor chipotle. Although mesquite is a smoke source in Mexico, we prefer the less greasy hardwoods. Mesquite charcoal (not briquets) is acceptable, especially when soaked hardwood chips are placed on top to create even more smoke. It is possible, however, that the resinous mesquite smoke (from the wood, not charcoal) contributes to the tan-brown coloration of the típico variety of chipotle.

Wash all the pods and discard any that have insect damage, bruises, or are soft, and remove the stems from the pods. Start two small fires on each side of the barbecue bowl, preferably using one of the recommended hardwoods. If you are using a meat smoker with a separate firebox, simply build the fire in the firebox and smoke the chiles until they are pliable but not stiff.

Place the pods in a single layer on the grill rack so they fit between the two fires. For quicker smoking, cut the pods in half lengthwise and remove the seeds. Keep the fires small and never directly expose the pods to the fire, so they won't dry unevenly or burn. The intention is to dry the pods slowly while flavoring them with smoke. If you are using charcoal briquets, soak hardwood chips in water before placing them on the coals, so the wood will burn slower and create more smoke. The barbecue vents should be opened only partially to allow a small amount of air to enter the barbecue, thus preventing the fires from burning too fast and creating too much heat.

Check the pods, the fires, and the chips hourly and move the pods around, always keeping them away from the fires. Be sure to stand upwind as you open the smoker; that smoke could be "hotter" than you think! It may take up to forty-eight hours to dry the pods completely, which means that your fire will probably burn down during the night and will need to be restoked in the morning. When

dried properly, the pods will be hard, light in weight, and reddish-brown in color. After the pods have dried, remove them from the grill and let them cool. To preserve their flavor, place them in glass jars.

Ten pounds of fresh jalapeños yields just one pound of chipotles after the smoking process is complete. A pound of chipotles goes a long way, as a single pod is usually enough to flavor a dish.

QUICK SMOKING

A quick smoking technique involes drying red jalapeños (sliced lengthwise, seeds removed) in a dehydrator or in an oven with just the pilot light on. They should be desiccated but not stiff. Then smoke them for three hours over fruitwood in a traditional smoker with a separate firebox, or in the Weber-style barbecue as described above. This technique separates the drying from the smoking, so you spend less time fueling the smoker.

Although jalapeños are the most popular chile for smoking, many people have started to smoke-dry a variety of peppers including habaneros, serranos, and even yellow wax varieties. Experiment with your favorite varieties, and you will be in for a real treat.

JALAPEÑO   HABANERO   SERRANO   YELLOW WAX

CHIPOTLES EN ADOBO

(SMOKED CHILES IN ADOBO SAUCE)

The word chipotle *generally means smoked chile and can be applied to any number of chiles treated that way in Mexico. In this recipe, however, use the smoked jalapeños. Use this as a cooking sauce or as an ingredient in barbecue sauces.*

12 dried **Chipotle Chiles**
1 medium **Onion**, sliced
3 cloves **Garlic**, sliced
3 cups **Water**
1/4 cup **Cider Vinegar**
1/4 cup **Tomato Sauce**
Salt to taste

Place all ingredients in a saucepan and simmer uncovered over low heat until the chipotles are soft, and the remaining liquid is reduced to about 1 1/2 cups. It will keep indefinitely in the refrigerator. It can also be made into a purée by blending the mixture in a blender or food processor.

Yield: 1 1/2 cups   *Heat Scale: Hot*

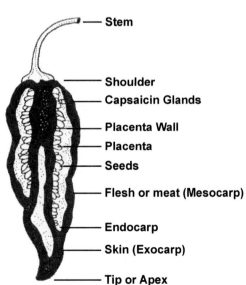

DIAGRAM
OF
A
CHILE

— Stem
— Shoulder
— Capsaicin Glands
— Placenta Wall
— Placenta
— Seeds
— Flesh or meat (Mesocarp)
— Endocarp
— Skin (Exocarp)
— Tip or Apex

CLASSIC CHIPOTLE HOT SAUCE

This is our version of the commercial Buffalo *chipotle sauce from Mexico. A tasty and easy way to reconstitute dried chipotle chiles is to place them in a bowl and cover them with cider vinegar. After several hours, the chiles will be reconstituted and will be plump.*

12 dried **Chipotle Chiles**, stems removed, reconstituted as above or soaked in **Hot Water** for 1 hour

1 medium **White Onion**, sliced

3 cloves **Garlic**, sliced

3 cups **Water**

1/4 cup **Cider Vinegar**

1/4 cup **Tomato Sauce**

Salt to taste

2 cups **White Vinegar** (more or less, depending on the thickness of the sauce you desire)

Drain the chiles. Combine all the ingredients except the 2 cups of distilled vinegar in a saucepan, cover, and simmer over low heat until the sauce is reduced to about 1 1/2 cups. Purée the mixture in a food processor or a blender until a paste-like mixture is achieved.

Combine the paste and the vinegar in a bowl and stir well. Strain through a sieve to remove the seeds and discard the solids.

Yield: About 3 cups   *Heat Scale: Hot*

CHIPOTLE

Hot, with a distinct smoky flavor, the chipotle is actually a dried, smoked jalapeño. The wrinkled skin of this chile ranges in color from dark brown to a light coffee tone. Chipotles can be found both dried or pickled.

W.C.'S CHIPOTLE SALSA

This is one of the three basic salsas served by our friend W.C. Longacre at his late, lamented Mountain Road Café. It is generally served as a dip with chips, but W.C. suggests spreading it over a grilled boneless chicken breast on a bolillo roll, topping it with grated mozarella cheese and popping it under the broiler until the cheese melts. A killer sandwich! This sauce will keep in the refrigerator for about a week and can be frozen.

12 **Chipotle Chiles**, stems removed, rehydrated in **Hot Water** for
   about 20 minutes
4 cups chopped, roasted and peeled **New Mexico Chile**
3 16-ounce cans **Tomatoes**, puréed
1 tablespoon **Salt**
1/4 cup **Sugar**
6 **Jalapeño Chiles**, stems and seeds removed, chopped
5 cloves **Garlic**, chopped
1/2 tablespoon **Powdered Garlic**
1/2 tablespoon **Old Bay Seasoning**
1/2 tablespoon **Honey**
1 tablespoon **Sesame Oil**
1/2 tablespoon **Mexican Oregano**
1/4 cup **Chipotle Barbecue Sauce** (see recipe page 74)

Drain the chiles. Combine, in batches, all the ingredients in a blender or food processor and pulse until the mixture is coarse with small chunks.

Allow to stand at room temperature for about 30 minutes to blend all the flavors.

Yield: About 3 quarts   *Heat Scale: Hot*

CHIPOTLE BARBECUE SAUCE

This is a basic "hot" barbecue sauce that goes well with poultry, as well as beef and pork. If you want more heat, add your favorite hot sauce or a couple of small dried chiles such as japones, piquins, or chiltepins. This sauce will keep in the refrigerator for about a week and can be frozen.

4 **Chipotle Chiles**, stems removed
1 tablespoon **Vegetable Oil**
1 medium **Onion**, chopped
1 clove **Garlic**, minced
1 cup **Ketchup**
1 tablespoon **Red Chile Powder**, **New Mexico Red** or **Ancho**
2 teaspoons **Dry Mustard**
3 tablespoons distilled **Vinegar**
3 tablespoons **Brown Sugar**
2 teaspoons **Worcestershire Sauce**

Rinse the chiles and cover them with very hot water and let them rehydrate and soften for at least 30 minutes. Drain the chiles and put in a blender or food processor along with a little water and purée.

In a large saucepan, heat the oil and sauté the onion and garlic until soft. Add the remaining ingredients, bring the mixture to a boil, reduce the heat, and simmer for at least 1 hour. Purée the sauce in a blender or food processor until smooth. Strain the sauce if desired.

Yield: 3 cups   *Heat Scale: Medium*

PIQUÍN

These tiny (about 1/2-inch-long) oval shaped chiles are a beautiful red-orange color when dried. They have a slightly sweet and smoky flavor and a fiery heat quotient. The wild form of the pequín is known as the *tepín* or *chiltepín*.

CHIPOTLE CHILE DIP CORDOBESA-STYLE

This smoky dip will amaze your guests. Serve it with fresh vegetables of your choice or with tortilla chips. This sauce will keep in the refrigerator for about a week and can be frozen.

4 ounces dried **Chipotle Chiles**, stems and seeds removed
1 cup packed **Brown Sugar**
Salt to taste
2 cups **Wine Vinegar**
1/3 cup **Olive Oil**
2 small **Onions**, chopped
1 head **Garlic Cloves**, peeled
1/2 teaspoon **Salt**
1/4 teaspoon **Thyme**
1/4 teaspoon **Oregano**
1 cup **Sour Cream**
1 cup **Mayonnaise**
1 tablespoon **Lemon Juice**
1 pound **Carrots**, peeled and cut into sticks
1 stalk **Celery**, cleaned and cut into sticks

Place the chiles, brown sugar, salt and 1 quart water in a saucepan and heat on low until the chiles rehydrate and the skin is easily loosened. Once the skins are removed, add the vinegar and stir. Remove the pan from the heat. In another pan, combine the olive oil, onions, garlic, salt, thyme, oregano, and sauté until the onions are soft.

Remove the chiles from the first pan and place in a blender or food processor with 1/4 cup of the liquid from the pan. Purée until smooth.

In a bowl, mix together the puréed chiles, onion mixture, sour cream, mayonnaise and lemon juice.

Serves: 10 to 12   *Heat Scale: Medium*

TOURNEDOS CON SALSA CHIPOTLE

(FILET MIGNON IN CHIPOTLE SAUCE)

This recipe, of Mexican origin from the state of Jalisco, is the fiery version of the famous Tournedos Béarnaise. We have provided a chipotle salsa, although any other chipotle sauce may be substituted. You can use the chipotles in adobo sauce or the dried ones.

THE SAUCE:

1 **Onion**, finely chopped
2 cloves **Garlic**
2 tablespoons **Oil**
6 dried **Chipotle Chiles**, soaked in water until soft, finely chopped
1 large **Tomato**, peeled, seeds removed, finely chopped
1/2 tablespoon **Dried Oregano**
1/2 teaspoon **Sugar**
Salt and **Pepper** to taste

THE TOURNEDOS:

4 **Tournedos**, cut from the best part of the filet mignon
4 slices **French Bread**, fried in **Butter** until golden brown

Sauté the onion and garlic in the oil until soft, then add all other ingredients and cook over a low heat until done, about a half hour. Remove from heat and purée in a blender or food processor until smooth. Return to the pan and keep warm until ready for serving.

Grill or sauté the tournedos to taste, usually rare or medium rare. Place each tournedo on a slice of toast, and spread the chipotle sauce over each. Serve warm.

Serves: 4   *Heat Scale: Medium*

SOUTHWESTERN SMOKY BAKED BEANS

Serve these as a hot replacement for traditional baked beans at your next picnic or barbecue. Any small white or haricot bean may be used in place of Great Northern beans. Use your favorite smoked chile powder or grind up some of your home smoked pods. Adjust the quantity used depending upon the variety of chile; for example, you wouldn't want to add an entire tablespoon of smoked habanero powder. If you are unable to obtain smoked powder, or cannot grind your smoked pods, simply soak a pod or two (again, depending on the variety) in some of the beer or water until soft. Then purée the chile in a food processor or blender before adding to the recipe.

- 2 cloves **Garlic**, chopped
- 1 tablespoon **Vegetable Oil**
- 1 tablespoon smoked **Chile Powder**
- 1/2 cup **Ketchup**
- 1/2 cup **Beer** or **Water**
- 1/4 cup **Dark Brown Sugar**
- 1 teaspoon **Dry Mustard**
- 1/4 teaspoon **Ground Cumin**
- 3 cups cooked **Great Northern Beans**
- 1/4 pound slab **Bacon**, cut into 1/2-inch pieces
- 1 large **Onion**, sliced and separated into rings
- 1 medium **Tomato**, peeled and chopped

Preheat the oven to 325 degrees F.

In a pan, sauté the garlic in the oil until soft. Combine the chile powder, garlic, ketchup, beer, sugar, mustard, and cumin in a bowl and stir to mix the flavors and to create the sauce. Layer the beans, bacon, onion and tomato in a baking dish and pour the sauce over the top.

Bake the beans for 2 hours or until the beans are tender and coated with the sauce. Add water if the mixture gets too dry.

Yield: 6 servings   *Heat Scale: Mild*

ANGRY PORK TENDERLOIN

Chipotles have remained an extremely popular chile, and our friend Chuck Evans provided this recipe. He manufactures six chipotle products under his Montezuma® Brand, and this recipe shows off the versatility of chipotle products.

1/4 cup **Classic Chipotle Hot Sauce**, p.*****
12 cloves of **Garlic** (yes, 12!)
3 **Shallots**, peeled
1 tablespoon ground **Allspice**
5 **Cloves**
1/2 cup **Malt Vinegar**
1/2 cup **Orange Juice**
1/4 cup **Lime Juice**
1/4 cup **Brown Sugar**
1 teaspoon freshly ground **Black Pepper**
1 1/2 cups **Olive Oil**

Place all ingredients except the olive oil and the tenderloins in a blender or food processor and puree, slowly drizzling in the oil. Marinate the meat in this mixture for at least an hour in a non-reactive bowl.

Grill the tenderloins over medium-high heat for about 8 minutes, turning every 2 minutes. Slice the tenderloins into 1/2-inch thick sections and serve with black beans, rice, salsa, and tortillas.

Yield: 4 servings   *Heat Scale: Medium*

SMOKY RANCH CHICKEN

Featuring W.C.'s Chipotle Salsa, this is quickly-prepared main dish. For the shortest preparation time, use already prepared ingredients and assemble in 10 minutes! When we have the time, we stew fresh chicken with onion, salt and pepper, using the meat and the broth.

Cooked shredded **Chicken** (4-6 cups)
2 cans condensed **Cream of Chicken Soup**
2 cups **Chicken Broth**
3/4 to 1 cup **W.C.'S Chipotle Salsa**, p. 00
1 4-ounce can can chopped **Green Chiles**
1 cup finely chopped **Onion**
1 to 2 dozen **White Corn Tortillas** cut into pieces
2 to 3 cups shredded **Monterey Jack Cheese**

Preheat the oven to 350 degrees. Lightly a grease 13" x 9" baking dish (or use cooking spray).

To make the sauce, combine the soup, broth and Salsa Verde in a bowl.

Assemble as follows in the baking dish.
- Thin layer of sauce on bottom of pan
- Layer of tortilla pieces
- Layer of chicken
- Layer of onion and chopped green chiles
- Layer of sauce (be generous)
- Layer of cheese

Repeat steps 2 through 6.

Bake for an hour uncovered. To serve, drizzle more Salsa Verde over top of casserole or serve as a side garnish.

Yield: 6 servings   *Heat Scale: Medium*

7 A PECK OF PICKLED PEPPERS

One of the best ways to handle an overwhelming chile crop is to pickle them. Pickling the peppers will preserve them at least until next year's crop comes in, and pickling makes "almost" fresh chiles available throughout the year. They can be pickled by themselves or in combination with other chiles or other vegetables. With just a little imagination, it's easy to turn out attractive, multicolored jars of pickled peppers. And, although pickling does require some time at the stove, it's an easy way to put up a lot of chiles.

PICKLING RULES

There are a few basic rules to follow when pickling:

1. Sterilize jars and lids in a boiling water bath for 10 to 15 minutes. We generally bring a large pot to a boil with an inch or two of water, along with a folded dish towel on the bottom of the pot. Jars are then placed, mouth down, into the water, along with the lids which can just be set between the jars. We then turn down the heat just enough to keep the pot slowly boiling or simmering.

2. Use pickling salt, rather than table salt which contains undesirable (for pickling) additives.

3. While cider vinegar is more flavorful, 5 to 6 percent distilled white vinegar should be used to avoid discoloring the chiles. Note that we do use cider vinegar when discoloration is not a problem.

4. Do not boil the vinegar for a long period of time as that will reduce the acidity.

5. Poke or cut a hole in each chile to keep it from floating and also to allow the pickling solution to work into the entire chile.

6. After filling each jar, remove any trapped air with a spatula or knife blade inserted between the chiles and the wall of the jar, or by gently tapping the jar.

7. After processing in a boiling water bath, remove jars to a draft-free location and allow to cool for 12 hours before handling.

PRESERVING IN ALCOHOL

One final method of "pickling" chiles is to preserve them in liquor. This method has several advantages to it, including the fact that the process can be completed without using the stove. Also, alcohol tends to change the chiles less than vinegar. Simply cut or poke a hole in each chile and cover with your preferred liquor. Vodka, gin, vermouth, and rum all produce tasty results. Not only does this process preserve chiles, it also produces some very interesting drinks!

PICKLED GREEN CHILE

These chile strips are great on sandwiches or when chopped and mixed with salads such as tuna or shrimp.

Note: This recipe requires advance preparation.

1/2 cup **White Vinegar**
1/2 cup **Sugar**
1 teaspoon **Pickling Salt**
1 teaspoon **Dill Seed**
1/2 teaspoon **Mustard Seed**
8 to 10 **New Mexico Green Chiles**, roasted and peeled, cut in strips (see Chapter 2 for roasting and peeling instructions)
3 cloves **Garlic**, cut in slivers

Combine the vinegar, sugar, and spices in a pan and simmer over low heat for 5 minutes. Put the chile into small, sterilized jars, cover with the liquid and add some garlic to each jar.

Cover tightly and refrigerate for 3 days before using.

Yield: 2 pints   *Heat Scale: Medium*

PICKLED PEPPERS

This recipe for approximately 2 pounds of peppers works well with jalapeños, serranos, yellow wax, cherry, habanero, or pepper-oncini chiles. So, if you're a lover of pickled peppers, mark this recipe as you'll be using it a lot.

Note: This recipe requires advance preparation and does not have to be processed in a water bath.

THE BRINE:

3 cups **Water**
1 cup **Pickling Salt**

Combine the salt and water and cover the chiles with the mixture. Place a plate on the chiles to keep them submerged in the brine. Soak the chiles overnight to crisp them. Drain, rinse well, and dry.

THE PICKLING SOLUTION:

3 cups **Water**
3 cups 5 to 6 percent **Distilled White Vinegar**
3 teaspoons **Pickling Salt**

Poke a couple of small holes in the top of each chile and pack them tightly in sterilized jars leaving 1/4-inch head space.

In a pan, combine the water, vinegar, and salt. Bring the solution to a boil and pour over the chiles, leaving no head space. Remove trapped air bubbles.

Store for 4 to 6 weeks in a cool, dark place before serving.

Yield: 4 pints *Heat Scale: Varies*

PICKLED HABANERO CHILES

To ensure the best pickled chiles, choose only the freshest ones and those with no blemishes. Bruised fruits will produce "mushy" chiles. You can also soak the chiles overnight in a brine of 3 cups water and 1 cup pickling salt to crisp them before pickling. Be sure to rinse them well to remove excess salt before processing.

Notes: This recipe requires advance preparation.

3 dozen fresh **Habanero Chiles** or enough to fill the jars
2 sterilized **Pint Jars**

THE PICKLING SOLUTION:

3 cups 5 to 6 percent **Distilled White Vinegar**
3 cups **Water**
1 1/2 teaspoons **Pickling Salt**

Poke a couple of small holes in top of each chile and pack them tightly in sterilized jars leaving 1/4-inch head space.

Combine the vinegar, water, and salt. Bring the solution to a boil and pour over the chiles. Remove trapped air bubbles by gently tapping on the sides of the jars. Add more of the pickling solution if needed; close the jars, leaving no head space.

Store for 4 to 6 weeks before serving.

Yield: 2 pints   *Heat Scale: Extremely Hot*

SUN-CURED PICKLED JALAPEÑOS

These pickled chiles have an East Indian flavor because of the mustard seeds and ginger. Any small green chiles can be substituted for the jalapeños. Serving suggestions: Serve these unusual chiles on sandwiches, hamburgers, or as a side relish for grilled or roasted meats.

Note: This recipe requires advance preparation.

- 1 cup **Jalapeño Chiles**, stems and seeds removed, cut in 1/4-inch strips
- 1 tablespoon **Pickling Salt**
- 1 tablespoon **Mustard Seeds**
- 1 teaspoon **Cumin Seeds**
- 1/4 cup **Oil**, **Peanut** preferred
- 1 teaspoon chopped fresh **Ginger**
- 1/4 cup freshly squeezed **Lemon Juice**

Sprinkle the chile strips with the salt; toss and let them sit for 10 minutes.

Toast the mustard and cumin seeds on a hot skillet, stirring constantly, for a couple of minutes until the seeds begin to crackle and "pop."

Heat the oil to 350 degrees F, remove from heat, stir in the ginger, then simmer it for 2 minutes. Remove the ginger and discard.

Stir in the chiles, mustard and cumin seeds and lemon juice. Pack in a sterilized jar.

For 5 days, set the jar in the sun in the morning on days when it is at least 70 degrees, and bring it in at night. Shake the jar a couple of times each day.

Yield: 1 pint   *Heat Scale: Hot*

HARVEST BOUNTY

This recipe can be used for pickling a combination of vegetables including chiles and bell peppers. Choose whatever mixture you desire, as well as the amount and type of chiles, and arrange them attractively in a jar before covering with the pickling solution. Be aware that some vegetables such as olives and mushrooms absorb capsaicin well and can become quite hot.

Note: This recipe requires advance preparation.

Chiles: Yellow Hots, Jalapeños, Serranos
Cauliflower, broken in flowerets
Broccoli, broken in flowerets
Zucchini, unpeeled and thinly sliced
Carrots, cut in coins or use baby **Carrots**
Pearl Onions, peeled and left whole
Garlic Cloves, whole
Small Button Mushrooms, whole
1/2 part **Water**
1/2 part **Vinegar**
1 teaspoon **Pickling Salt** per pint of liquid

Wash the chiles and prick with a toothpick. Arrange your choice of vegetables and chiles in sterilized jars.

Bring the water, vinegar and salt to a boil and allow to boil for one minute. Pour over the vegetables, leaving no head space, and cover.

Allow the mixture to pickle for at least 2 to 3 weeks in a cool, dark place before serving.

Yield: Varies   *Heat Scale: Varies*

ITALIAN GIARDINIERA

This basic recipe can be used for pickling chiles either alone or with a combination of other vegetables. Choose the mixture of vegetables desired, the amount and type of chiles, and arrange them attractively in a jar before covering with the pickling solution.

Note: This recipe requires advance preparation.

> **Fresh Chiles** of choice. Wash them and, with a toothpick, poke several holes near the stem before packing in the jars
> 1/2 part **Water**
> 1/2 part **Vinegar**
> 1 teaspoon **Pickling Salt** per pint of liquid
> **Cauliflower**, broken in flowerets
> **Cucumbers**, unpeeled and cut in chunks
> **Onions**, cut in wedges
> **Garlic Cloves**, whole
> **Green Olives**

Wash the chiles and prick with a toothpick. Arrange your choice of vegetables and chiles in sterilized jars.

Bring the water, vinegar and salt to a boil and allow to boil for one minute. Pour over the vegetables, leaving no head space, and cover.

Allow the mixture to pickle for at least 2 to 3 weeks in a cool, dark place before serving.

Yield: Varies   *Heat Scale: Varies*

SUMMER SQUASH PICKLES

This recipe calls for zucchini, but yellow squash or cucumber will work just as well.

1 pound fresh **Zucchini**, unpeeled and cut in thin slices
2 **White Onions**, thinly sliced and separated into rings
1/4 cup **Pickling Salt**
6 small hot fresh **Chiles**, such as **Serrano** or **Cayenne**, stems removed, cut in half
1/2 cup **Cider Vinegar**
1/2 cup **Lemon Juice**, fresh preferred
4 cloves **Garlic**, sliced
2 tablespoons **Sugar**
2 teaspoons **Celery Seed**
2 teaspoons **Yellow Mustard Seeds**
1 teaspoon **Dry Mustard**

Place the squash and onions in a colander and sprinkle with the salt and let sit for 1 hour. Rinse well and drain.

Pack the vegetables into sterilized jars along with the chiles.

Combine the remaining ingredients in a pan, bring to a boil and pour over the vegetables, leaving 1/4-inch head space. Adjust the lids and process in a boiling water bath for 10 minutes.

Yield: 2 pints   *Heat Scale: Varies*

SPICY PRESERVED ONIONS

Spicy onions are a welcome change from plain ones. Serve with sandwiches, hamburgers, hot dogs, or as a condiment. They are especially good with tacos and fajitas.

Note: This recipe requires advance preparation.

    3 pounds **White Onions**, thinly sliced
    1 small **Carrot**, peeled and thinly sliced
    6 **Serrano Chiles**, stems removed, chopped, or substitute other hot
        fresh chiles

THE PICKLING SOLUTION:

    3/4 cup **White Vinegar**
    3/4 cup **Water**
    1/4 cup **Sugar**
    10 **Whole Black Peppercorns**
    6 whole **Cloves**

Pour boiling water over the onions and carrots and let sit for 1 minute. Drain and layer in sterilized jars along with the chiles.

Bring the remaining ingredients to a boil in a pan and pour over the onion mixture, leaving no head space, and cover.

Allow the onions to marinate for a couple of days in a cool, dark place before using.

Yield: 4 pints   *Heat Scale: Mild*

SERRANO

A small (about 1 1/2-inch-long) slightly pointed chile with a very hot, savory flavor. As the Serrano matures, its smooth, bright green skin turns to scarlet red, then yellow. Serranos are available fresh, pickled or packed in oil.

PICKLED GREEN BEANS

Putting up chiles with other prolific vegetables such as green beans, takes care of two "too many" crops at one time. These spicy beans are a great addition to an appetizer tray.

Notes: This recipe requires advance preparation.

2 pounds fresh **Green** beans, left whole
12 fresh **Red Chiles**, left whole, such as de arbol, cayenne or Thai
6 cloves **Garlic**
1 cup chopped **Onions**
1 1/2 tablespoons **Dill Seeds**
2 teaspoons **Black Peppercorns**
3 cups **White Wine Vinegar**
1 cup **Water**
2 tablespoons **Sugar**
1/2 teaspoon **Pickling Salt**

Trim the ends off the beans and remove the strings. Cook the beans in boiling water until barely tender, 3 to 5 minutes. Drain and plunge beans into ice water to stop cooking.

Stand the beans up in sterilized, wide-mouthed jars. Divide the chiles, garlic, onions, dill, and peppercorns among the jars.

Combine the vinegar, water, sugar, and salt in a pan, bring to a boil, and pour over the beans.

Seal the jars and allow to sit for a couple of weeks in a cool, dark place before serving.

Yield: 6 pints   *Heat Scale: Varies*

JALAPEÑOS EN ESCABECHE

Escabeche *means "pickled" in Spanish, and this recipe is a way of pickling chiles that is popular in Mexico and other Latin countries. This particular method requires that the peppers be cooked and packed with several other vegetables. A variety of small hot chiles can be used, so don't limit yourself to only jalapeños.*

Note: This recipe requires advance preparation.

> 1 pound **Jalapeño**s, whole
> 1/4 cup **Olive Oil**
> 1 medium **Onion**, thinly sliced
> 2 small **Carrots**, thinly sliced
> 4 cloves **Garlic**
> 12 black **Peppercorns**
> 1/4 cup **Pickling Salt**
> 3 cups **White Vinegar**
> 3 cups **Water**

In a pan, sauté the chiles in the oil until the skin starts to blister. Add the onion and carrots and heat for an additional minute.

Pack the chile mixture into sterilized pint jars leaving 1/2-inch head space.

Add a clove of garlic, 3 peppercorns, and 1 teaspoon salt to each of the jars.

In a pan, combine the vinegar and water and bring to a boil. Pour over the chiles.

Seal and process the jars in a boiling water bath for 15 minutes.

Store for 4 weeks in a cool, dark place before serving.

Yield: 4 pints   *Heat Scale: Medium*

SPICY RED WINE VINEGAR

Many creative chefs have herb gardens. An herb garden doesn't need to be large or elaborate to produce fresh herbs that are such a treat; extra herbs can be microwaved until dried and stored for later. Once you get hooked on making different herbal vinegars, you'll want to expand your knowledge of herb gardening.

> 3/4 cup fresh **Basil Sprigs**, washed and patted dry
> 3 to 7 small, **Hot Red Chiles** (such as piquin or chiltepin), depending on your desired heat level
> 1 pint of good quality **Red Wine Vinegar**
> 1 **Non-metallic Bottle**, slightly larger than a pint

Place the basil and the chiles in a non-metallic saucepan. Pour in the vinegar and heat, but do not boil. Let the mixture cool slightly and pour it into the non-metallic bottle. Cover the top loosely (again, nothing metallic), and let the mixture steep for 10 days.

Yield: slightly more than 1 pint   *Heat Scale: Varies with the number of chiles*

CHILTEPINS IN ESCABECHE

In the states of Sonora and Sinaloa, fresh green and red chiltepins are preserved in vinegar and salt. They are used as a condiment or are popped into the mouth when eating any food—except, perhaps, oatmeal. Since fresh chiltepins are not available in the U.S., adventurous cooks and gardeners must grow their own. The tiny chiles are preserved in three layers in a 1 pint, sterilized jar. Note: This recipe requires advanced preparation.

> Fresh red and/or green **Chiltepins** (as many as you want to pickle)
> 3 cloves **Garlic**, peeled
> 3 teaspoons **Salt**
> 3 tablespoons **Cider Vinegar**
> **Water** as needed

Fill a 1-pint jar 1/3 full of Chiltepins. Add 1 clove garlic, 1 teaspoon salt, and one tablespoon cider vinegar. Repeat this process twice more and fill the jar to within 1/2 inch of the top with water. Seal the jar and allow to sit for 15 to 30 days.

Yield: 1 pint   *Heat Scale: Very hot*

8. CREATIVE PRESERVATION

There are a good number of non-traditional ways to use even more of your overabundant harvest, in combinations as diverse as hot chile vinegar, cilantro-chile butter, and jalapeño jelly.

CHILE VINEGARS

Chile vinegars are a great way of utilizing some of the chiles that are left after drying, freezing, and pickling your crop. Use these flavored vinegars for marinades, with oil for salad dressings, or to deglaze pans. We have included a couple of recipes, but use your imagination in combining your favorite herbs with chiles and vinegar, using the basic instructions as a guideline.

This is probably the easiest way to put up chiles. Simply pack the chiles and herbs in sterilized jars and cover with the vinegar. Place the jars in a cool, dark place and leave undisturbed for three to four weeks. Strain the mixture.

Note: You may speed up the process by heating the vinegar and pouring it over the herbs, which have been chopped and crushed. Let the mixture steep for a couple of days before straining and rebottling.

ROSEMARY CHILE VINEGAR

This is our favorite vinegar. Recommended chiles include serranos and habaneros, but it can also be made with dried pasillas for a raisiny flavor.

Note: This recipe requires advance preparation.

    2 tablespoons minced fresh small **Chiles**
    1 cup fresh **Rosemary Leaves**
    3 peeled **Garlic Cloves**, left whole
    1 quart **White Vinegar**

In jars, cover the chiles, rosemary, and garlic with the vinegar and cover. Place the jars in a cool, dark place and leave them undisturbed for three to four weeks. Strain, pour into clean, sterilized bottles, and label them.

Yield: 1 quart   *Heat Scale: Varies*

OREGANO GARLIC GREEN CHILE VINEGAR

The combination of oregano and garlic imparts an Italian flavor to this vinegar, which we keep on the mild side, so that the heat doesn't mask the flavor of the garlic.

Note: This recipe requires advance preparation.

    1 cup fresh **Oregano Leaves**
    10 peeled **Garlic Cloves**, left whole
    2 fresh **Green Chiles** such as **Serrano** or **Thai**, cut in half
       lengthwise
    1 quart **White Vinegar**

Cover the oregano, garlic, and chiles with the vinegar in a large jar. Store in a cool, dark place and leave the jar undisturbed for three to four weeks. Strain and pour into clean, sterilized bottles.

Yield: 1 quart   *Heat Scale: Mild*

CHILE OILS

Any of the preceding vinegar recipes can also be used to make flavored oils. Be aware that fresh herbs will cloud the oil as they break down, so remove them as soon as the flavor has developed. Basil is the worst offender and will turn black in the oil. If using garlic, thread the cloves on wooden skewers because if a fuzzy haze develops around them, they need to be removed and removing a skewer is easier than removing individual cloves.

ASIAN CHILE OIL

Bottles of chile oil decorated with ribbons and tiny papier-mâché chiles make nice gifts for anyone who likes to cook. Include an oriental stir-fry recipe along with each gift bottle.

Note: This recipe requires advance preparation.

    1 cup small dried **Red Chiles**, such as piquíns
    4 cups **Vegetable Oil**, **Peanut** preferred

In a pan, heat the oil to 350 degrees F, remove from the heat, and add the chiles.

Cover the pan and let stand for 12 to 24 hours (the longer it steeps, the hotter the oil). Strain the oil into clean, sterilized jars or bottles.

Tie a few dried chiles to the jars for decoration.

Yield: 4 cups   *Heat Scale: Hot*

SICHUAN GINGER OIL

This oil adds a lot of flavor to any dish, especially oriental fare, but don't limit its use. It's also great on a simple salad of mixed greens and bean sprouts.

Note: This recipe requires advance preparation.

- 2 cups **Vegetable Oil**, **Peanut** preferred
- 2-inch piece fresh **Ginger**, sliced
- 3-inch **Cinnamon Stick**
- 4 small dried **Red Chiles**, such as **Piquín, Thai,** or **Cayenne**
- 1 teaspoon lightly crushed **Sichuan Peppercorns**

Heat the oil to 350 degrees F in a saucepan. Remove from the heat, add the remaining ingredients, and let the oil cool.

Cover the pan and let stand for 12 to 24 hours (the longer it steeps, the hotter the oil). Strain the oil and pour into clean, sterilized jars.

Yield: 2 cups   *Heat Scale: Mild*

PIRI-PIRI OIL

This interesting sauce is the Caribbean oil-based variation on the African sauce from Angola, which was transferred to the region by Portuguese immigrants working the cacao plantations in Trinidad and Guyana. Use it to spice up soups and fried fish. Pimento leaves are traditionally used in this recipe, but they are hard to find.

Note: This recipe requires advance preparation.

- 3 cups extra virgin **Olive Oil**
- 2 **Habanero Chiles**, cut in half
- 1 teaspoon **Lemon Zest**
- 2 bay **Leaves**

Combine all ingredients in a jar and seal tightly. Place the jar in the refrigerator and let steep for 2 weeks. Remove the top and stir every 2 or 3 days. The longer it steeps, the hotter it will become.

Yield: 3 cups   *Heat Scale: Hot*

FLAVORED LIQUORS

This method is the opposite from preserving chiles in alcohol; we are adding flavor and heating up the liquor.

PEPPER VODKA

Pepper vodkas are very popular in Russia and also among our vodka-loving friends. The longer the chiles are left to steep, the hotter the vodka; so if you are giving this as a gift, adjust the heat to the taste of the recipient. This is great to use in Bloody Marys.

Note: This recipe requires advance preparation.

4 **Jalapeño Chiles**, seeds and stems removed, quartered
1 quart **Vodka**

Place the chiles in the vodka and let sit for a week or more. Remove the chiles (if desired) and serve.

Yield: 1 quart   *Heat Scale: Varies*

BIRD PEPPERS IN SHERRY

This recipe, which we found in a 1940s Trinidad cookbook, is probably one of the earliest methods of flavoring sherry in the tropics. It is also called "pepper wine." The sherry, which gradually picks up heat from the bird peppers, is sprinkled into soups and stews and makes them quite exotic. The peppers can be either fresh or dried.

Note: This recipe requires advance preparation.

20 **"Bird Peppers"** (**Chiltepins**), stems removed
1 bottle **Dry Sherry**

Add the peppers to the sherry and allow to steep for several days in the refrigerator.

Yield: 1 bottle   *Heat Scale: Hot*

TEX-MEX LIQUORS

Chiles and cumin combine here to create the olfactory essence of the Border. Most any type of small, dried chile pepper that you can get in the bottle will work. Be sure to taste it often, and remove the chiles when it reaches the desired heat. Serve extremely cold, over ice or in tomato juice for an "instant" Bloody Maria. Flavored liquors are often prepared in the Southwest with sliced jalapeños.

Note: This recipe requires advance preparation.

> 4 to 6 dried **Chiltepin Chiles**, left whole (or substitute piquíns)
> 1 teaspoon **Ground Cumin**
> 1 liter **White Tequila**

Place the chiles and cumin in the tequila and let them steep for a week or more. Periodically taste the liquor, and remove the chiles when the desired heat has been obtained.

Yield: 1 liter   *Heat Scale: Varies, but usually hot*

CHILE CONDIMENTS

Virtually any condiment you can think of can contain chiles—sometimes in fairly large quantities.

JALAPEÑO MUSTARD

Replace mundane, yellow mustard with this spicy version. Use a chile/herb vinegar for an even hotter, more flavorful mustard. For a smoother mustard, grind all the seeds to a fine powder.

Note: This recipe requires advance preparation.

- 1/2 cup **Yellow Mustard Seeds**
- 3/4 cup **Yellow Mustard Powder**
- 1 cup **Flat Beer**
- 1/3 cup **Vinegar**, **Cider** or **Chile Herb Flavored**
- 1/2 teaspoon **Salt**
- 4 **Jalapeño Chiles**, stems and seeds removed, minced

Grind one half of the mustard seeds to a fine powder. Coarsely grind the remainder of the seeds.

Combine the mustard seeds and powder, beer, vinegar, and salt and mix well. Stir in the chiles and pack into clean, sterilized jars.

Allow the mustard to sit in a cool, dark place for 2 weeks before using. Be sure to refrigerate after opening.

Yield: 1 pint   *Heat Scale: Hot*

FIERY FRUIT CHUTNEY

Chutney are the Indian version of a highly seasoned relish or ketchup and are usually sweet and spicy. Serve this one as an accompaniment to shrimp, poultry or curries.

- 1 cup **Pitted Prunes**, chopped
- 1 1/2 cups **Cider Vinegar**
- 1 tablespoon **Lime Juice**
- 1 cup **Brown Sugar**
- 1 teaspoon **Dry Mustard**
- 1 teaspoon **Ground Cinnamon**
- 1/2 teaspoon **Salt**
- 1/4 teaspoon **Ground Cumin**
- 1 cup **Seedless Raisins**
- 6 small fresh **Red Chiles**, such as **Cayennes** or **Serrano**s, stems and seeds removed, chopped
- 2 cups chopped **Tart Apples**
- 1 cup chopped **Onions**
- 1 cup peeled, chopped **Tomatoes**

Cover the prunes and raisins with very hot water and let steep for 10 minutes to soften. Drain.

Combine the vinegar, lime juice, sugar, mustard, cinnamon, salt, and cumin in a large kettle and bring to a boil. Add the prunes, raisins, chiles, apples, onions, and tomatoes. Cover and boil the mixture, stirring frequently, for 20 minutes or until the mixture has attained the desired consistency.

Pour into clean, sterilized jars and seal.

Yield: 2 pints   *Heat Scale: Medium*

JALAPEÑO JELLY

This jelly goes well on crackers with cream cheese or as a basting sauce for grilled poultry.

8 **Jalapeño Chiles**, stems and seeds removed
2 medium **Green Bell Peppers**, stems and seeds removed
1 1/4 cups **White Vinegar**
1/4 cup **Lemon Juice**
5 cups **Sugar**
6 ounces **Liquid Pectin**
Green Food Coloring

Place the jalapeños and bell peppers in a blender or food processor and pulse, being careful not to chop the peppers too finely.

Combine the vinegar, lemon juice, and sugar in a large kettle and bring to a rolling boil. Add the chiles and bell peppers, along with any juice, and boil rapidly for 10 minutes, stirring occasionally and removing any foam that forms. Add the pectin and food coloring. Bring back to a boil and while stirring constantly, boil for an additional minute.

Skim off any foam that forms and bottle in clean, sterilized jars.

Yield: 5 cups   *Heat Scale: Hot*

JALAPEÑOS & SERRANOS

COMPOUND BUTTERS

Compound butters are a combination of herbs, spices, and butter that can be used in a variety of ways—on vegetables, potatoes and pasta, with grilled meats, poultry, or fish. Use these butters for sautéing foods or even cooking an omelet. They will keep indefinitely in the freezer, so make several variations to keep on hand.

ORANGE ZEST RED CHILE BUTTER

Serve this on breakfast toast.

- 2 tablespoons grated **Orange Zest**
- 2 teaspoons **Orange Juice**
- 2 teaspoons **Ground Red Chile**, such as **New Mexico**, **Piquîn**, or **De Arbol**
- 1 teaspoon **Onion Powder**
- 1 pound **Unsalted Butter**, softened

Mix all the ingredients together and allow to sit at room temperature for an hour to blend the flavors. Wrap in plastic or wax paper and freeze.

Yield: 1 pound   *Heat Scale: Varies*

DE ARBOL

Known as the "tree chile" in Mexico because the bush resembles a small tree. The hot pods are red and about one-quarter inch wide by one and a half to three inches long. Also called *pico de pájaro* (birds beak), *puya, cuauhchilli, alfilerillo* and *cola de rata.*

CINNAMON CHIPOTLE CHILE BUTTER

This butter adds a great touch to vegetables, fish, and even a grilled steak.

1 medium **Chipotle Chile**, stem and seeds removed
2 teaspoons **Ground Cinnamon**
1 pound **Unsalt**ed **Butter**
2 teaspoons **Lime Juice**

Cover the chipotle with very hot water and let sit until soft, about 30 minutes. Drain the chile and place in a blender or food processor along with some water and purée until smooth.

Mix all the ingredients together and allow to sit at room temperature for an hour to blend the flavors. Wrap in plastic or wax paper and freeze.

Yield: 1 pound   *Heat Scale: Medium*

About the Authors

Dave DeWitt is one of the foremost authorities in the world on chile peppers and spicy foods. In the late 1970s, Dave researched and wrote numerous magazine and newspaper articles on chile peppers. His first cookbook, *The Fiery Cusines*, co-authored with Nancy Gerlach was published in 1984.

Dave was the editor-in chief of *Chile Pepper* magazine which he, Nancy and a local publisher launched in 1987. In 1997, Dave launched *Fiery Foods & Barbecue Business Magazine,* a trade publication. In 2001, that magazine was re-launched as *Fiery Foods & Barbecue* magazine, a consumer publication.

Dave has written 31 books and continues to write at the rate of one or two books a year. He is also producer of Albuquerque's National Fiery Foods & Barbecue Show, now in its fourteenth year.

Nancy Gerlach is a Registered Dietition, and has been involved in all aspects of the food industry. She is recognized as one of the premier authors in the U.S. on the subjects of chile peppers and fiery foods. Nancy was the founding food editor of *Chile Pepper Magzine,* a position she held for 10 years and is the current food editor for *Fiery Foods and Barbecue* magazine. She has written a wide variety of articles for many national publications and developed literally thousands of recipes which have been tested, so that any home cook can easily reproduce them.

Jeff Gerlach is an expert gardener, specializing in chiles, and a cookbook author.

Other Books by Dave DeWitt & Nancy Gerlach

The Fiery Cuisines
Fiery Appetizers
The Whole Chile Pepper Book
Just North of the Border
The Habanero Cookbook
Heat Wave: The Best of Chile Pepper Magazine
The Pepper Pantry: Habaneros
The Food of Santa Fe
Barbecue Inferno